Striper
Hot Spots

"Here's a mini-Baedecker detailing 100 prime shoreside locations . . . Daignault's new effort will provide valuable information for all who plan visits to the great northeastern striper grounds."

—Frank Woolner
Editor Emeritus, *Salt Water Sportsman*

"In this comprehensive directory, Daignault has divulged the real secrets of the striper old-timers."

—Jerry McKinnis
Producer, ESPN "The Fishin' Hole"

Also by Frank Daignault

Twenty Years on the Cape: My Time as A Surfcaster
Striper Surf

STRIPER HOT SPOTS

The 100 Top Surf Fishing Locations
from New Jersey to Maine

Second Edition

by Frank Daignault

The Globe Pequot Press

Old Saybrook, Connecticut

Library of Congress Cataloging-in-Publication Data
Daignault, Frank.
    Striper hot spots : the 100 top surf fishing locations from New Jersey
to Maine / by Frank Daignault. — 2nd ed.
      p.   cm.
    ISBN 1-56440-994-5
      1. Surf fishing—Atlantic Coast (New England)—Guidebooks.
    2. Striped bass fishing—Atlantic Coast (New England)—Guidebooks.
    3. Surf fishing—New Jersey—Atlantic Coast—Guidebooks. 4. Striped
    bass fishing—New Jersey—Atlantic Coast—Guidebooks. 5. Atlantic
    Coast—(New England)—Guidebooks. 6. Atlantic Coast—(N.J.)—
    Guidebooks. I. Title.
    SH464.A85D35 1996
    799.1'66145—dc 20
                                                    96-23060
                                                    CIP

Manufactured in the United States of America
Second Edition/Second Printing

Contents

v

New Jersey

	RATING (OUT OF 🐟🐟🐟🐟🐟)	INLET FISHING	JETTY FISHING	FLY FISHING	OVERSAND VEHICLE ALLOWED	OVERSAND VEHICLE NECESSARY
1. Cape May	🐟🐟🐟	X	X			
2. Hereford Inlet	🐟	X	X			
3. Townsend's Inlet	🐟🐟	X	X			
4. Corson's Inlet	🐟	X			X	
5. Absecon Inlet Plus	🐟🐟	X	X			
6. Brigantine Inlet	🐟🐟	X		X		X
7. Beach Haven Inlet	🐟🐟🐟	X		X	X	
8. Long Beach Island	🐟🐟		X		X	
9. Barnegat Inlet South Jetty	🐟🐟🐟	X	X			
10. Barnegat Inlet North Jetty	🐟🐟🐟	X	X			X
11. Sedge Island	🐟🐟	X		X		
12. Island Beach	🐟🐟				X	
13. Manasquan Inlet	🐟	X	X			
14. Manasquan to Long Branch	🐟🐟🐟		X			
15. Sandy Hook Point	🐟🐟🐟	X	X	X		

#	Location	Fish	Col 1	Col 2	Col 3	Col 4
41.	Weekapaug Breachway	🐟 🐟	✗	✗	✗	
42.	Quonochontaug Breachway	🐟 🐟 🐟 🐟	✗	✗	✗	✗
43.	East Beach	🐟 🐟				✗
44.	Charlestown Breachway	🐟 🐟 🐟 🐟	✗	✗	✗	
45.	Deep Hole	🐟 🐟 🐟			✗	
46.	Harbor of Refuge	🐟 🐟 🐟 🐟	✗	✗	✗	
47.	Point Judith	🐟 🐟	✗	✗		
48.	Narragansett's Rocky Shore	🐟 🐟 🐟				
49.	Narrow River Inlet	🐟 🐟 🐟	✗		✗	
50.	Conanicut Island (Beavertail)	🐟 🐟				
51.	Barrington River	🐟 🐟	✗		✗	
52.	Warren River	🐟 🐟	✗		✗	
53.	Bristol Narrows	🐟 🐟	✗		✗	
54.	Brenton Point State Park	🐟				
55.	Fort Adams State Park	🐟				

	RATING (OUT OF 🐟🐟🐟🐟🐟)	INLET FISHING	JETTY FISHING	FLY FISHING	OVERSAND VEHICLE ALLOWED	OVERSAND VEHICLE NECESSARY
Block Island						
56. Southwest Point	🐟🐟🐟					
57. Mohegan Bluffs	🐟🐟🐟					
58. Southeast Light	🐟					
59. Grove Point	🐟🐟					
60. Inlet to Great Salt Pond	🐟🐟🐟🐟	X	X	X		
Martha's Vineyard						
61. Vineyard Bridges	🐟🐟🐟🐟	X	X	X		
62. Wasque Point	🐟🐟🐟🐟🐟					X
63. Squibnocket Point	🐟🐟🐟🐟🐟					
64. Gay Head Cliffs/ Pilots Landing	🐟🐟🐟🐟					
65. Lobsterville Beach and Jetty	🐟🐟🐟	X	X	X		

	RATING (OUT OF 🐟🐟🐟🐟)	INLET FISHING	JETTY FISHING	FLY FISHING	OVERSAND VEHICLE ALLOWED	OVERSAND VEHICLE NECESSARY
77. Nauset Beach	🐟🐟🐟🐟	X		X		X
78. Chatham Inlet	🐟🐟🐟🐟	X		X		X
79. Chatham Inlet/South Island	🐟🐟🐟🐟	X		X		
80. Nauset Inlet	🐟🐟🐟🐟	X		X	X	
81. Outer Cape	🐟🐟🐟🐟					
82. Provincelands	🐟🐟🐟			X		X
83. Race Point	🐟🐟🐟🐟			X		X
84. Pamet River	🐟🐟🐟	X	X	X		
85. Sandy Neck Beach	🐟🐟	X		X		X
86. Hull Gut	🐟🐟	X				
87. Boston North Shore	🐟🐟🐟	X		X		
88. Plum Island	🐟🐟🐟🐟	X	X	X		

New Hampshire

89. Hampton River Inlet	X	X
90. General Sullivan Bridge/ Great Bay	X	

Maine

91. Mousam River	X	X
92. Saco River	X	X
93. Old Orchard Beach		
94. Scarborough River Marsh	X	X
95. Spurwink River	X	X
96. Martin Point Bridge/ Presumpscot River	X	
97. Popham Beach	X	X
98. Morse River	X	X
99. Kennebec River	X	X
100. Penobscot River	X	X

Acknowledgments

While I claim full credit for the formulation of this book's concept, purpose, and execution, there are any number of contributors without whose able assistance *Striper Hot Spots* would never have come to be. Early in the project, I sought the help of some trusted friends on the Striper Coast. In exchange for their familiarity with certain sections of the shore, I promised each of them a coffee-table copy of the finished work and a guaranteed mention of their contribution within its pages to show their grandchildren; in addition, they have the knowledge that they contributed something to a sport I was already certain they loved. South to north, please applaud the following:

Ed Bronstein of Fin-Atics in Ocean City and Gary Gibson of Sea Island City submitted their knowledge of South Jersey. Morris "Black Cloud" DeGenarro, with his forty-two years of surfcasting experience, sacrificed a few minutes of fishing to tell us about that fine stretch from Beach Haven Inlet to Barnegat Light. Steven Perna brought his youthful vitality to the project by giving us the inside story on Island Beach State Park (hot spots 10, 11, and 12) and then editing the final product for the perfection that he demonstrates in everything he undertakes. I also thank Jack Bennet and John Chiola, who took time from the manufacture of their fine lures to expose North Jersey's finest fishing and even sent a runner to count all 121 jetties in number 14. Most of all, they kept the ball rolling by putting me in touch with "Black Cloud."

The western Long Island section would have never been possible without Chet Wilcox and Richie Altenkirch. East Hampton's George Campbell and his wife, Claire, gave me Orient Point, enabling me to stretch Long Island to a reasonable number of spots, what with the inaccessibility of the North Shore. Without Amagansett's Captain Harvey Bennett, Montauk—for all its standing as a surfcasting mecca—

would have remained shrouded in mystery for this writer. And I would have found none of these people without Russ Drumm of the *East Hampton Star.*

I am also grateful to Captain Ray DeCosta for his lifetime of experience on Nantucket, and I owe a debt to Bill Pew for many of the details there that I never thought to ask DeCosta about. If there was a Nantucket book, they could have coauthored it.

Kay Moulton of Surfland Newburyport rattled off the whole story on Plum Island; what a racket I could have had with ninety-nine more like her.

The late Dr. Robert Post, author of that fine treatise on the Vineyard's legendary surf fishers, *Reading the Water,* didn't just tell me about fishing there, he wrote about it. Another professional writer, and faithful longtime friend, Matt Zajac, penned much of the material on Connecticut. Then, Ron Rozsa, a biologist for Long Island Sound Programs, and Rod Macleod, a biologist for Connecticut Marine Fisheries, wrapped that state up, all three assuring me that their participation was a privilege. Dick Pinney of the *Manchester Union Leader,* looking at the back of his hand to conjure up New Hampshire's hot spots, rattled them off like the names of his children.

Lastly, Billy Gardner of Portland gave me half of Maine and corrected any errors that I might have made from my own research there. Even my daughter, Susan Daignault, who is now a Mainer, led me to Fort Popham long before this book's conception. All these people have been the cat's meow.

It will surprise no one from the beaches and gun clubs of New England who knows me that my wife, Joyce, rules upon everything written here from the initial concept to its final execution. Imagine having a high school sweetheart who becomes your wife, lover, companion in the woods and on the beaches, and mothers four beautiful children for you along the way. Then, just when you think it can't get any better, she assists in the production of one's books. What a joy she has been for our forty years together. Scary that I need her so much.

Here's one of seven 50-pound-plus linesides that I have taken in my forty years of surfcasting experience. (1966 photo)

Introduction

The purpose of this book is to document the one hundred finest surf-casting locations on the Striper Coast, from the south end of New Jersey to central Maine. It is a directory of prime places to go fishing. It contains directions, geographic considerations, fishing methods in use, and favored angling times. There are, of course, any number of shore-fishing locations outside these parameters, but I have chosen these because social and natural considerations render them the most reasonable.

The main criteria for the selection of these hot spots are their productivity and accessibility. I define *productivity* here as a surfcaster's potential for success as compared with other locations. Success, of course, can be based upon the catching of any number of gamefish, and these can be ranked according to species most often sought, those most important. The guiding considerations here, which should surprise no seasoned saltwater angler, are, in rank order: striped bass, bluefish, weakfish, blackfish, fluke, cod, bonito, and porgy. While this leaves out some species, I think the spirit of my intent has been served. Of course, if stripers were the only game in town, this book would be limited to them alone. Indeed, with some exceptions, if it isn't a striper spot, it doesn't count. But so often, a place that appeals to one fish appeals to another, as is the case when adding bluefish and weakfish. Similarly, some locations where the striper is locally important have a unique run of another species and the secondary gamefish is often overlooked; still another is famous for blackfish but overlooked for its fine striper fishing. I have tried to cover all that is known.

What this book is *not* is a treatise on surfcasting. You are expected to have learned that elsewhere, or to be engaged in the lifelong pursuit of this knowledge. You are supposed to know how to deal with slick jetties and sloppy salt-chuck—often green, white, and dirty—blowing over the jetty, which is the only thing between you and your maker. Calkers, cleats, belts, flotation, and judgment are outside the bounds of this book. *It is assumed that you know that surfcasting can be quite dangerous.*

It is not enough to list a hundred places without extensive supportive information. Techniques and conditions play no small part in the formulation of a hot spot, as well as what is needed to make it all work. The selection of technique becomes a case of choosing between what one thinks is best versus what is being done locally. I tend to go with the latter, on the assumption that the anglers who frequent a spot know more than I about what works there. No seasoned regular would argue that most places enjoy sets of favored conditions that often improve or ruin the fishing. For instance, a sou'west wind at Race Point during a given stage of tide might enhance one's opportunities; conversely, an east wind might ruin all hope on a particular east-facing beach—though not on all east-facing beaches. To make matters more complicated, there might even be an interrelationship between methods and conditions: for example, if everybody says that pink Nockajimas work best at a given place during a southeast wind, that is the way it gets written up.

Another consideration for inclusion here is that it has never been our intent to document some little hot spot that accommodates two esoteric hardcores doing a striper number alone in the dark of night. Not because secrecy is important or that I take anyone's threats seriously, but such disclosures would serve no purpose. As a result, public property predominates (94 percent of hot spots) because of its inherent accessibility. Conversely, some places are more popular than they deserve to be simply because they accommodate greater numbers of fishermen.

When I take into account all the factors—size, accessibility, species availability, water movement and depth, facing directions, and overall production in terms of fish caught—each hot spot begs for some sort of value judgment that defines it more objectively. Indeed, to keep the information that gathers on a particular spot in control, a rating system serves as a means of boiling it all down. Here, I must quickly create a clear separation between a 5-mile hot spot at the mouth of a river, like Plum Island, and some obscure beach a mile long that is rarely fished—and all the levels in between. What springs from those thoughts is that Montauk Point is rated a five while "Little Beach" is a one. Of course, such judgments can become mighty subjective while inspiring heated disagreements—as often based on local pride as on protectionist sentiments. With those thoughts in mind, I am tempted to apologize in advance for decisions that might seem skewed to some knowing regular out there. My rating system breaks down as follows:

Rating	Number of Hot Spots
⟩ ⟩ ⟩ ⟩ ⟩	7
⟩ ⟩ ⟩ ⟩	22
⟩ ⟩ ⟩	31
⟩ ⟩	29
⟩	11

If I dare believe that this book will enjoy any life after its initial release, I must take into account the influence of time upon species. All gamefish are inexorably destined to rise and fall in availability as years go by. Certainly, striped bass—at this writing—are at heretofore unknown levels of high population, due to some lucky reproductive seasons, better management, and restoration efforts. Bluefish, I have learned through extensive examination of historical accounts, seem to be subject to fifty-year cycles. In the 1960s, many surfcasters could not identify one, but by the 1970s, blues were seen in Maine for the first time in one hundred years. It is known that a species extends its range only when at a peak in its population, and while there is no need to elaborate further about today's bluefish angling opportunities, I must emphasize that those opportunities have never remained historically constant, nor will they.

In my lifetime, I have seen the rise and subsequent fall of gray weakfish (*Cynoscion regalis*) twice. The reasons cited for this variation include natural cycles and overfishing. They are now at a relative low in their cycle and are rare in the northern part of their range but increasing in New Jersey. By contrast, variations in the blackfish population seem far less dramatic. While the above examples make the point, I will date myself here by saying that fluke, or summer flounder, are in decline . . . again; black sea bass are coming back; scup are as thick as insects; and cod and pollock are so over-fished commercially that they are rare at the beach, whereas at one time I used to catch them all winter in the surf. My point here is that just because a species is listed at a spot does not mean that it will be available the year you happen to fish there. I am, however, tempted to say that there will always be something, because it appears that the demise of one species seems always to be a signal for the advance of another. Even the bait species, so central to each creature's existence, experience rises and declines in population; this implies some larger cyclical pattern for everything living in the ocean, but adequate explanation is still elusive. I hasten to underscore that baitfish cycles have a direct bearing on the behavior of those species we seek.

This book contains four distinct kinds of information: (1) observations that are entirely my own and for which I bear sole responsibility, as with the stretch from Watch Hill to Race Point; (2) information that is a combination of personal experience and research, in which I depended upon some input from others, such as with Maine; (3) sections that are completely the result of research, for which I began by interviewing qualified respondents and then checked the information for accuracy, as with New Jersey, Long Island, and Nantucket; and (4) sections that were written by others and then reviewed by me, as is the case with Martha's Vineyard and some parts of Connecticut. As one might guess, the greatest danger lies with outside input, which was occasionally colored by evasive tactics to protect a spot.

One of my fears is that some of this fact distortion could have slipped through. Not so much that a spot might have been skipped because apparently cooperative advisers were steering an agenda, but, rather, because surfcasters were out to protect their home turf. Indeed, out and out refusal to cooperate would have been more welcome, and I had some of that.

Block Island got more protection than it deserved. That was in keeping with the overt behavior by its protectors that has characterized it since its discovery as a viable, though often overstated, striper hot spot. Smashed windshields and slashed tires in the past have too many people running scared, while others suggest that bypassing the

Block entirely would be safer. Of course, its obvious omission would have been tantamount to encasing it in neon and would have brought it to the attention of every surfcaster this side of Australia. There was so much stonewalling that my first investigation was rendered worthless. After a second examination of Block Island, I still don't trust the information, partly because no one was willing to risk mention of his or her name in the acknowledgments section here. What few remember and most never knew is that the first article I ever published, "Block Island Safari" (*Salt Water Sportsman,* August 1970), expounded upon the great bluefishing from shore there at a time when the species was still quite scarce, as well as the suspicion that bass fishing was not exactly shabby when productive striper fishing was discovered in Mohegan Bluffs in July of '69. So much for secrecy.

Striper Hot Spots is nothing more than some badly needed musical chairs that engages the same number of seats while changing the rumps. This broadening of people's available locations will have no adverse influence upon the quality of the sport. Yet, there were actually people who sought to protect "Mourn-talk" by playing it down and/or asking me not to include it. As though a hole in Connecticut's shoreline chain link fence were going to leak a few thousand interlopers onto the Orient Point ferry, when Point Judith or the Cape Cod Canal would be easier and closer. Like the Lower Bronx Striper Slaughter Association never heard of Long Island, that it has an end, and that it comprises public property, namely Montauk. But—get ready for this—protection and secrecy for Montauk from a bait-and-tackle shop?

Conversely, I had one guy who swore that a well-known nearby bastion of striper fishing had only "passing" fish that were on their way to their ultimate location, the river behind his bait shop, where he could provide bait for them and coffee and sandwiches for you and me. It started to sound good until he told me that the first stripers arrive there—at the northmost end of their range—in late March. Fishing starts there *as a trickle* May 15.

Of course, the above incongruities get more attention than they deserve, as they make interesting reading and serve as a study in

human chicanery, but they are not representative. Nearly all (nineteen out of twenty) to whom I spoke were truthful, said so when they didn't know, and told me where I could find out. They were usually thrilled to participate in this endeavor, which should certainly outlast me and probably some of them. Smart enough to know, without being reminded, that they were contributing something, they were enthusiastic, truthful, and flattered to have the opportunity.

Examining some of the common qualities of the one hundred locations yielded some not-so-surprising statistics. For instance, 63 percent of them are inlets. I have long said, always practiced, and on many occasions written on the beauty of inlets as places where bait lured great gamefish. Because so many inlets are flanked by jetties to preserve their integrity, 31 percent of the spots ended up being flanked by jetties. That 54 percent of the spots host fly fishing speaks more of the trendy nature of the activity. Truth is that one could fly fish them all, but I tried to stay with either personal experience or that of respondents. The use of oversand vehicles is permitted in 28 percent of the places, but that is not to say that a "beach buggy" is needed to fish there in all cases. They are truly necessary for only ten spots on the Cape and islands, and just two in New Jersey.

This revised edition drops Colt Drive in Rhode Island because officials close the park at sunset. Cuttyhunk is still pleasant but loses out because of travel hassles. Pilgrim Nuclear Plant presents security, and as a result, access problems. And, Bailey's Island, Maine just couldn't hold up to the standard because of bluefish in decline. To replace these, Troy and Enfield dams offer exciting opportunities; Chatham Inlet, now split, refines the best in this directory; and the Boston North Shore, with the help of Pete Koutrakis, fills a void. Block Island's Inlet to Great Salt Pond bumps nearby Charlestown Beach through a badly needed change in emphasis. We are now facing the inlet side of the breakwater. A dozen other spots have been rewritten extensively with more pertinent information. And, in response to the overwhelming interest in fly fishing, we have made a greater effort to identify the growing list of suitable fly-fishing locations. Fly fishers should watch for the special fly icon, which designates hot spots known for fly fishing. Lastly, instead of a non-fishing activity that appeared in the first edition, each of the 100 hot spots has either a contact tip—a fishing shop you can call—or a cogent fishing tip that can help you while fishing.

The hot spots are listed in geographical order, from south to north, as the migrating species travel. So if you don't like to read a book in order, or if you just plain like to jump around, feel free to do that here.

NEW JERSEY

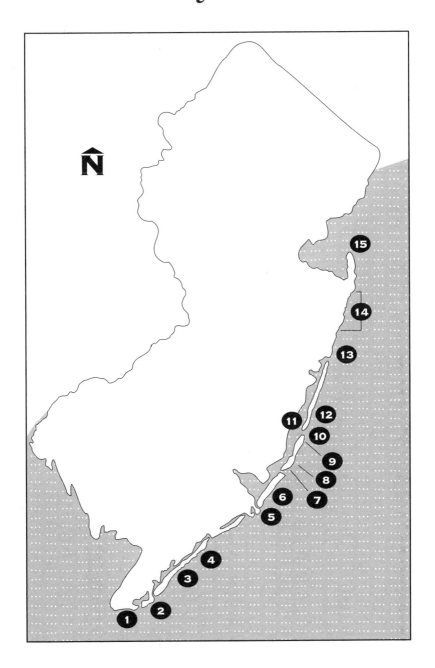

Who says New Jersey is the Garden State? It should be known as the Jetty State.

A sk any Massachusetts linguist and he'll tell you that Jersey people talk funny. I can attest to that from my youthful days, when I would hear the serious Jersey surfcasters say that "the boids is woikin'." But what I remember most about them is that after driving hundreds of miles to a Cape Cod beach, they could never take time out to sleep or eat without feeling a certain guilt. For them, having reached the pinnacle of surfcasting opportunity demanded total devotion and allowed no time for creature comforts. One thing I've always known is that there are few casual surfcasters.

Morris "Black Cloud" DeGenarro is one of those people, and I've known a hundred like him in my lifelong tenure on the Striper Coast; he is so passionate about his success as a surfman that, while he focuses on his goodness, he overlooks his greatness. "Black Cloud," as he has come to be known in North Jersey because of a propensity for bringing changes in the weather, is one of those delicious people who knows just enough about fishing the beach to gain your trust quickly. The inscrutable quality that DeGenarro exudes is one of eternal optimism, a quality I have observed in many of the best fishermen I have known—and no small number of them have been Jersey surfmen visiting New England beaches. For instance, when I asked DeGenarro about Hole Gate (hot spot number 7), I sought to exact from him a best tide for the fishing there. I could tell from his hesitation, the obvious drift of his mind, that to choose a best tide would have forced him also to consider a worst tide. To DeGenarro, that is an unacceptable set of choices; to someone like him, nothing that has to do with surfcasting can be anything but great. His thinking—if I dare seek to examine the nobility in anyone, let alone a surfcaster—has no place for bad fishing. He is incapable of casting aspersions on something to which he has so great a commitment. Thus, while I seek to draw from his experience, I must never forget that it is not his knowledge that might flaw him as a source of information but rather his inscrutable faith that all tides are good and that there are no ill winds—the failing of optimists everywhere. I choose him to teach by example that there may be more hope here than truth in some cases, more enthusiasm than fact. Black Cloud is thus enigmatic in the sense that he is precisely something other than what his nickname implies. The truth is that he personifies the universal belief among anglers that one more great fish swims for just one more cast.

Lest I be accused of spending more time in the examination of Jersey's people than its fishing, I must note that I was struck by a number of that state's geographical features. It is, above all, a place of countless jetties; so much so that surfcasting has come to mean jetty fishing in the shore-fishing mind there. Another observation I made is that the farther north one went in the Garden State, the better the striper fishing. It is widely believed in the state that being nearer to the Hudson River—a major source of East Coast stripers—can do nothing but help. There are notable climatic differences in New Jersey waters that influence those species found in its surf. For example, you won't find puppy drum north of here, and only an occasional kingfish will visit waters above Long Island, whereas they can be found in nuisance numbers in South Jersey. Unaccountably, porgies—known as scup where I fish—are viewed as an offshore species. And while I examine predatory species, it is only reasonable to note that forage here is different from that found farther north on the Striper Coast. Anglers who baitfish with a live spot in Jersey would find no such bait available above Montauk, and only the most astute Rhode Island observer would even be conscious of a fall mullet run in his state, while it is a major natural event in New Jersey. Crabs and clams are popular striper bait in South Jersey, yet never used for linesides in Massachusetts or Rhode Island.

Lastly, I must acknowledge that the per capita number of surf fishermen in this state is surely the largest of any state on the Striper Coast. On Thanksgiving morning of '91—and this is a holiday celebrated by nearly all Americans, a day that custom and tradition acknowledge as one of the most significant family holidays of the year—there was no room to stand or fish among the 3,000-plus surfcasters lined up on Island Beach . . . at (are you ready?) 4:00 A.M.

1

Cape May

BEST MONTHS TO FISH: April through December.

RECOMMENDED METHODS: Lures and baits.

FISH YOU CAN EXPECT TO CATCH: Bluefish, weaks, kingfish, flounder, and stripers.

HOW TO GET THERE: At the end of the Garden State Parkway, go straight south over the bridge into town. The names change—Lafayette, West Perry, Sunset Boulevard—but it's a straight run. Follow the signs to Cape May Point State Park.

In the vicinity of Cape May Point and Lighthouse, there are eight jetties, any of which can produce suitable fishing for just about every species listed for this area. Farther west, there is another, less popular, group of jetties. Those fishing "the point" like to see a northeast wind, because it piles up water, bait, and gamefish along this part of the shore. Tidewise, there are individual preferences, but most to whom I spoke said they liked the outgoing tide. No doubt, this preference takes into account that during a moon tide a nor'easter will cover most of the jetties with dangerous foam, making it about impossible to fish many of them. Outgoing tides are safe, as it is unlikely to get worse.

Cape May Inlet, which is guarded on both shores by fishable jetties, is probably the best of it, but the military keeps both sides under tight control. The south jetty is accessible only to Coast Guard personnel, and the north is closed to vehicles unless the owner has a military I.D. (which includes military retirees and those with a red Reserve card). Diehards walk the 2 miles when striper fishing heats up—which can be any time, but more likely late fall. I'm told that the north jetty is worth the walk.

Methods vary more widely here because of the variety of species involved; thus, details for each of the less glamorous species are being bypassed to say more about stripers. Plug fishing is just as popular here as elsewhere and remains the center of interest. However, the fall mullet run finds many anglers using actual mullet or plug imitations. Live eels are another choice that is distinctive in that the smaller "whip" eels, rated at thirteen to the pound, are often used with light tackle. At an average of an ounce and a quarter each, these small baits are drifted along the jetty edges.

CONTACT TIP: Inquire about Cape May at Rodia's Bait and Tackle, (609) 886–0505.

2

Hereford Inlet

North Wildwood, New Jersey

BEST MONTHS TO FISH: April through December.

RECOMMENDED METHODS: Lures and baits.

FISH YOU CAN EXPECT TO CATCH: Bluefish, weaks, kingfish, flounder, stripers, and occasional puppy drum.

HOW TO GET THERE: Take Garden State Parkway exit 4 to Route 47 east.

Two of the eight jetties on the south side of Hereford Inlet are sanded in, but the others provide opportunities for all species in season. Most popular are the Surf Avenue and New York Avenue jetties. As with Cape May, northeast winds are popular, and slack tides at both ends seem to be what anglers wait for. The exception seems to be flounder fishermen, who like high tides. Better opportunities for kingfish, I'm told, are in the back, the more estuarine part of the inlet; regulars use bloodworms or shrimp on the bottom. Crossing the two ocean bridges, drive north to the back, where there are wadable marsh areas; it is possible to plug light gear or fly fish during the night for school striper fishing, which is mostly catch-and-release fishing. While there are two main channels at this writing, the inlet is largely sanded in and doesn't exchange as much water as many other inlets on this coast.

CONTACT TIP: Gibson's Tackle can inform you about the fishing at Hereford Inlet. Call (609) 884–2248.

3

Townsend's Inlet
Sea Isle City and Avalon, New Jersey

BEST MONTHS TO FISH: April through December, but fall is best.

RECOMMENDED METHODS: Big plugs, rigged eels, and live baits that represent what is available—mullet, eels, and pogies.

FISH YOU CAN EXPECT TO CATCH: Stripers, blues, kingfish, fluke, and blackfish.

HOW TO GET THERE: From the Garden State Parkway, take exit 13 to Avalon for the south bank, exit 17 for Sea Isle City on the north bank.

There is no favored side to Townsend's Inlet, where anglers line up to cash in on the currents flowing from behind the barrier beach. Though there are no actual inlet jetties, there is a rockline on the south side. There are, however, some true jetties on the south side in Avalon. The Eighth Street jetty is popular, because it is both long and easy going with cement filling the cracks. On some evenings or early dawns, the fishermen lined up here look like a fence line from a distance.

Currents are strong at the inlet itself with some anglers prefer-ring an hour each side of the slack in tide. Falling tides should be better than the rise, but whenever water isn't suitable at the inlet, it is possible to work the many jetties. As in much of South Jersey, when stripers and blues are slow during the summer, they are com-pensated for by the other, less glamorous, species. There is good blackfish (tog) under the bridge on the south side. As the ap-proaches are township land, there are no access problems, but day parking in summer can be tough. All of this area is highly accessible by car, but after September 15, you can use a buggy.

CONTACT TIP: Call Fin-Atics, (609) 398–2248, in Ocean City to learn about current action at Townsends.

4
Corson's Inlet (Strathmere Inlet)
Strathmere, New Jersey

BEST MONTHS TO FISH: April through December.

RECOMMENDED METHODS: Small plugs and lures or bottom baits.

FISH YOU CAN EXPECT TO CATCH: Kingfish, fluke, stripers, and bluefish.

HOW TO GET THERE: From the Garden State Parkway, take the Ocean City exit (Route 52). Follow the shore road, Ocean Drive, for about 7 miles to the toll bridge. (An oversand ve-hicle is recommended.)

What with the new toll bridge, the old bridge to Strathmere is now a fishing pier that is run by the state. Nearby parking is part of a state park, so there are no hassles. This is a popular daytime spot for easy-to-catch eating fish like weaks, kings, and fluke. Corson's is not a favored striper hot spot when compared to most of the other listings, but I'm sure that at times they must be available there in the night. Particularly in the fall, bluefish would be surprised to find that they are listed last here. This is a good spot to bring the kids to fish, since there are safe railings on the bridge and there is good protection from a sea storm here.

CONTACT TIP: Gibson's Tackle, (609) 263–6540, in Sea Isle City can report on Corson's Inlet fishing.

5

Absecon Inlet Plus
Atlantic City, New Jersey

BEST MONTHS TO FISH: October through December.

RECOMMENDED METHODS: Plugs and free swimming live baits, including eels.

FISH YOU CAN EXPECT TO CATCH: Stripers and bluefish.

HOW TO GET THERE: Follow the Atlantic City Expressway right into Atlantic City, then take Atlantic Avenue to a right onto New Hampshire; take a left 2 blocks down onto Oriental, which leads to the inlet and the T-jetty.

The first four jetties on the south side of Absecon Inlet are a popular collection of jetties right in Atlantic City that produce stripers on a regular basis. Naturally, those nearest the inlet enjoy better current. The T-jetty, which best borders the inlet, is used regularly and is flat and easy. Keep in mind that flow in this area causes the north sides of rock piles to be deeper. While both sides of the jetty on the Brigantine side are fished, the north side seems to have an edge in spite of better currents on the south.

Back in Atlantic City, the Vermont Avenue jetty (south side) is the spot where Albert McReynolds landed a 78½-pound striper in the early '80s for an All-Tackle World Record. His accomplishment played some part in the rating of this area; however, the intense tourism of summer, coupled with crowds of transient people, raises the specter of security difficulties, just about ruling out summer fishing for the lone surfcaster in the deep of night. This is, after all, the city.

CONTACT TIP: Call Atlantic City Fishing Center, (609) 344–4778, for information.

6

Brigantine Inlet

Brigantine, New Jersey

BEST MONTHS TO FISH: April through December.

RECOMMENDED METHODS: Plugs, eels, bottom baits, and fly fishing.

FISH YOU CAN EXPECT TO CATCH: Stripers, bluefish, weakfish, kingfish, and flounder.

HOW TO GET THERE: Follow the Atlantic City Expressway into Atlantic City, then take Ohio and Huron avenues to Route 87 and follow signs to Brigantine. Northbound on Brigantine Avenue leads to the inlet.

The long, slow curve of Brigantine Inlet is all sand. Because there are no jetties, bottom sand shifts as the product of a season's winds and currents, and it is a perfect spot for reading the many shallow sloughs and holes that develop there. Again, northeast winds are popular, even though they are in your face here, and dropping tides seem to draw available fish to these shallows. It may be more important to fish at night here, however, because stripers are often reluctant to risk shallow water without the cover of darkness. The

In order to get the most out of Brigantine Inlet, you should have a buggy. Big bluefish like this one are common in the fall.

premise that night fishing is basic to surf fishing is all the more important in shallow locations like this one. Also, don't hesitate to fly fish the back for smaller fish—at night.

The distance from hard top to inlet is about ¾ mile; however, the town does issue permits to drive the beach with a buggy.

CONTACT TIP: Chestnut Neck Boat Yard, (609) 652–1119, usually knows area action.

7
Beach Haven Inlet (Hole Gate)
Beach Haven, New Jersey

BEST MONTHS TO FISH: April through December.

RECOMMENDED METHODS: Lures and baits; some fly fishing.

FISH YOU CAN EXPECT TO CATCH: Stripers, bluefish, weaks, kingfish, and flounder.

HOW TO GET THERE: Take exit 63 off the Garden State Parkway, then go east on Route 72 to Ship Bottom. Turn right (south) onto Long Beach Boulevard and proceed about 10 miles; you'll find the inlet. (Oversand vehicle is helpful after September 15).

The inlet at Beach Haven is one of the region's best shore fishing hot spots. While any of the last 3 miles will produce all species, the nearer you go to the end, with its currents, the better your chances are of finding suitable fishing. With so much flow from Little Egg Harbor, it is not necessary to restrict your fishing to any particular tide. Regulars all claim that they do as well on the upcoming water as on the drop. As with the more southerly Jersey areas, the north-easter is a popular wind, and the nor'wester helps the cast when the angle of this beach is considered. A popular way to fish stripers, blues, and weaks here is to utilize a mullet rig bottom fishing. This is a pin harness with a small cork float that lifts the bait off the bottom to avoid scavengers. Earlier in the season, before mullet present themselves, chunks—bunker or mackerel—can be used on the bottom.

Methods, hook size, bait, time of day, and season determine what species are likely, though I admit to frequent surprises. Small offers take fluke, kingfish, and smaller weaks; big plugs or eels cull out small stuff in favor of bigger stripers when they are around, and they are most often around in the fall. Don't overlook the more protected back estuary if you like fly fishing.

With the required town permit, beach buggies may be used starting September 15. Locals wait for that date because it enables them to drive the last ½ mile to the inlet until May 15. They walk it in warmer months.

CONTACT TIP: The Ancient Mariner in Beach Haven, (609) 492–0269, is up to date.

8

Long Beach Island
New Jersey

BEST MONTHS TO FISH: April through December, but fall is best.

RECOMMENDED METHODS: Lures and baits.

FISH YOU CAN EXPECT TO CATCH: Stripers, bluefish, weaks, kingfish, and flounder.

HOW TO GET THERE: Take exit 63 off the Garden State Parkway, then go east on Route 72 to Ship Bottom.

This entire 12-mile stretch entertains migrating schools of game-fish. Because of the shore road here, it is possible to drive the entire island to locate schools of fish feeding along the shore. The whole island is laced with jetties, but these are low and unsuitable for walking or crawling, as they often flood; however, they still draw migrants at both ends of the season because of the cover they offer.

Bluefish are the most likely to be seen, but by November expect schools of bass as well, which can last late into December. A widely held belief is that the later it is in the season, the more likely one is to find action in the daytime. Still, if linesides are around, and you can take the water temperatures, night remains prime. Plugs and lures are best in the fall because of the mobility that goes with using them. It should be noted that after Labor Day it is possible to acquire a beach buggy permit (about $60) for all the towns from Harvey Cedars south.

CONTACT TIP: To inquire about Long Beach Island, call Bruce and Pat's, (609) 494–2333.

9

Barnegat Inlet South Jetty
Barnegat Light, New Jersey

BEST MONTHS TO FISH: April through December.

RECOMMENDED METHODS: Lures and baits.

FISH YOU CAN EXPECT TO CATCH: Stripers, bluefish, weaks, king-fish, flounder, and blackfish.

HOW TO GET THERE: Take exit 63 off the Garden State Parkway, then go east on Route 72 to Ship Bottom. Take a left (north) onto Long Beach Boulevard and follow for 8-plus miles to Barnegat Light.

Three years in the making, the new South Jetty was completed in 1992. At this writing it remains unknown just how good this 3,224-foot-long jetty is going to be for fishing. It is so new, and so flat, that you don't need cleats. There is even a handrail for the first 1,000 feet. This is all public property and there are no parking hassles.

Opinions about this spot were beginning to emerge just as I wrote this: The end of the jetty is preferred; the dropping tide is best, particularly low slack when big stripers shift positions. Weakfish are more likely on the south, or outside, of the rocks, stripers more likely on the north, or inside, where the serious currents are. When fishing for blackfish, remember that they are more likely to be found at the jetty base near the rocks. Outside of the mullet season, a deadly bait for bass are calico crabs or soft shedder blue claws; split the big ones to create a scent. This spot is among the best-in-state, with anglers lined up on both sides of Barnegat Inlet.

CONTACT TIP: For Barnegat Inlet information, call Fisherman's Headquarters, (609) 494–5739.

10

Barnegat Inlet North Jetty
Island Beach State Park

BEST MONTHS TO FISH: May, June; September through December.

RECOMMENDED METHODS: Live bait and swimming plugs.

FISH YOU CAN EXPECT TO CATCH: Stripers, bluefish, weakfish, fluke, and blackfish.

HOW TO GET THERE: Take exit 82 off the Garden State Parkway, then Route 37 east to Tom's River and Seaside Heights. Follow signs to Island Beach and drive south the entire 11½-mile length of this barrier beach island to arrive at Barnegat Inlet.

It is 1½ miles on foot from the southernmost parking area to the jetty. Stretching southeast from the beach, the jetty is over 200 yards long; it can be wet (depending on the wind), and spikes or corkers are needed along with full foul-weather suiting. The dropping tide is popular here along the inlet side of the jetty. When fishing the ocean side of the jetty, however, an incoming tide is preferred. There is an excellent pocket where jetty joins beach that locals run to when the wind is north or nor'east. Best striper fishing is at both ends of the season, with July and August avoided by most. As with all of Jersey, the September mullet run triggers a fall heat-up of stripers, blues, and weakfish. But note that fluke and, to some degree, weakfish augment summer fishing enough to fill out the calendar.

Oversand vehicles are commonly used to cover the last stretch from the parking lot. A permit is required, along with the usual equipment: jack, shovel, board, air gauge, tow rope. There are three-day permits for those visiting and an annual permit, which costs $125 at this writing.

CONTACT TIP: The Hook House, (908) 270–3856, knows about this area.

11

Sedge Island
Barnegat Bay
Island Beach State Park

BEST MONTHS TO FISH: Late April through August.
RECOMMENDED METHODS: Sand crabs, alewives, bucktails, plugs, fly fishing, and swimming plugs.

FISH YOU CAN EXPECT TO CATCH: Stripers, bluefish, weakfish, and fluke.

HOW TO GET THERE: Take exit 82 off the Garden State Parkway, then Route 37 east to Tom's River and Seaside Heights. Follow signs to Island Beach and proceed south to Barnegat Inlet.

Sedge Island offers protected estuarine fishing.

This protected estuarine spot is in the back of the last parking area, but access from there is difficult. Most people get to "the Sedge" by walking from the inlet toward the back bay. Less of a walk than to the North Jetty, what anglers call "Sedge Island" is really not the island itself but a strip of land toward the island in the rip between the barrier beach and island. The narrow passage of water between the barrier and the island is the big appeal. The outgoing tide is best. During the higher stages of tide, there is also some excellent flats-wading where plugs or flies can be used in the deep of night. Because of its protected nature, this spot is a lifesaver when the front beach is getting a pasting from a storm. When baitfishing for blackfish, use the sand crabs and pick the rocky areas.

TIP: Stripers are most vulnerable to flies when feeding on sperling or sand eels.

12
Island Beach
Island Beach State Park

BEST MONTHS TO FISH: May and June, and September through December.

RECOMMENDED METHODS: Live bait, all plugs, and lures.

FISH YOU CAN EXPECT TO CATCH: Stripers, bluefish, weakfish, fluke, and blackfish.

HOW TO GET THERE: Take exit 82 off the Garden State Parkway, then Route 37 east to Tom's River and Seaside Heights. Follow signs to Island Beach.

The beach fishing portion of the whole Island Beach State Park can be fished best when an oversand vehicle is used. That is not to say that a buggy is required, because a car can be utilized on the road paralleling the beach, but a buggy enables a surfcaster to view the entire 8-mile waterline in spring and fall and much of it during the summer. Also, one can make the most of mobility by utilizing plugs or lures. Fall fishing is what Jersey hungries all wait for.

Of course, you can locate migrating fish anywhere, but two areas, places where regulars go first, stand out, and after viewing them, you'll understand why. Island Beach utilizes a system of marking beach locations, A-1 to A-23, each about ¼ mile from the next one. The stretch from A-6 to A-13 is a garland of structure where beach readers will go out of their heads with excitement. While most of this is off limits to beach vehicles during the summer, access by foot from the parking lot is open year-round. This stretch of bars, sloughs, and holes is open to driving from October 1 on—just in time to catch the fall madness.

Write this down: A-6 to A-13.

Three miles south of the entrance to the park, the first buggy access, called Gilliken's Road, is another blow-your-mind location for all but the least knowledgeable. For a mile south from Gilliken's, you'll see a highly readable structure of rips, bars, and pockets. Again, you don't have to have a buggy: just drive into one of the pull-offs and walk over the dunes. Collections of buggies—if the whole beach isn't a mass of them—often mean something. Back at the Gilliken's Road access, a lot of regulars will park their buggies and walk north because of the nice cover that borders the surf there. My hunch is that the driving prohibition keeps headlights off the water enough to lure greater numbers of gamefish into the shallows. Surfcasters hate leaving their rigs, so it has to mean something if they are willing to walk north when they could drive south for up to 8 miles.

Coming into Island Beach on the right, you have to pass Betty and Nick's Bait and Tackle, which is run by Frank Mazza. As with so many other shops on the Striper Coast, this "information central" maintains a log book of who, what, when, where, and how.

Making the log is what it is all about for many, but you might want to use some discretion about the how and where.

CONTACT TIP: Betty and Nick's Bait and Tackle, (609) 793–2708, knows the score for Island Beach.

13

Manasquan Inlet
Brielle/Point Pleasant, New Jersey

BEST MONTHS TO FISH: April through December.

RECOMMENDED METHODS: Drifting live baits, plugging, and eels with tin squids.

FISH YOU CAN EXPECT TO CATCH: Stripers, bluefish, and weakfish.

HOW TO GET THERE: From the south on the Garden State Parkway, take exit 88 and Route 88 (same numbers) to Point Pleasant, then head north on Route 35. If you're coming from the north, leave the Parkway at exit 98 for Route 35 south to Brielle.

The two jetties flanking Manasquan Inlet are fished with equal zeal and both enjoy public access and parking, provided that surfcasters go there at night. Customary day use of the beach fills the parking lot quickly. The big method here is to drift either live or dead spot or snapper blues. Naturally, if you have live ones and can keep them, you'll have an edge. Remember to watch for the early fall mullet run, which is a sign that swimming plugs often do the trick. Come November, everything works.

Best tide is the outgoing, but once it slackens regulars head for where the Point Pleasant Canal runs into the Manasquan River.

CONTACT TIP: Alex's Bait and Tackle, (908) 295–9268, is right near the inlet.

14

Manasquan to Long Branch (Jetty Country)
New Jersey

BEST MONTHS TO FISH: May through December.

RECOMMENDED METHODS: Live baits, big swimmers, calico crabs, and tin squids.

FISH YOU CAN EXPECT TO CATCH: Stripers, bluefish, and weakfish.

HOW TO GET THERE: Go east on any of the Parkway exits from Manasquan to Long Branch; they will lead to suitable shore roads that are available the full length of this stretch.

Anybody from outside this North Jersey area would be over-whelmed by the thought of 121 jetties in a 20-mile stretch of shoreline. Of course, the count—done by the hangarounds of J&J Tackle, in Belmar—includes every string of stones, about one-third of which are not likely to produce a whole lot of striper fishing. Still, some of the eighty or so "good ones" are big and easy, luring stripers of all sizes. I must also take into account that some rock piles are more accessible than others, and parking varies from jetty to jetty. (Note that meters are policed all night in Belmar.) John Chiola tells me that occasionally somebody comes along to challenge the right of anglers to fish certain jetties, but they always lose. Let's go fishing.

There is a good string of ten or more jetties in Spring Lake, but you can't get on all of them at the top of the tide. Consequently, regulars will wait for the water to lower before trying them. Because they cover, you can be sure the rocks will be slick. Area regulars have their favorites, which serve to fill the night with

The stretch from Manasquan to Long Branch has more jetties than any like stretch of shore I've seen. These hungries won't miss a drift.

opportunity; they know which ones will be productive while they wait for others to be exposed by the tide. And, within each jetty, they know the lies that stripers like to use. It is a certainty that each place that has ever given up a fish is indelibly stored in their memory. Naturally, there is a certain competition among regulars to be the first to check a spot during a favored phase of tide. Exactly what tide phase is best for a particular location is usually a closely guarded secret, but often known by more than one angler. Catches and near misses reduce the chances of following anglers; poorly shielded lights send stripers that might be there hell west, and even the click of cleats upon the stones might be enough to spook a lineside out of there. Thus, efforts to be the first on a rock pile, to reap the benefits of virgin territory, are no small part of the local cult. As I find myself saying more about the surfcasters than the surf fishing here, it is my hope that new anglers can draw a number of cogent lessons: first, that jetty fishing is a specific discipline under the greater god of surfcasting, and that it is, as a result, more dangerous, more demanding than those other shore fishing situations with which you may be confronted elsewhere; second, that most jetty anglers have paid their dues with a lifetime of sleepless nights or lost jobs and have experienced the variety of social turmoil one might expect from spending one's nights at the shore instead of tending to normal business. Nothing shuts up a battered and bruised surfcaster more quickly than somebody who is asking a lot of questions and seeking a free ride on the coattails of that kind of history. This North Jersey territory is steeped in surfcasting tradition, and its jetties are no small part of it. Thus, anyone aspiring to become part of this exclusive corps would do well to prove his or her worth in the same hard way.

It improves from Manasquan north to a peak of opportunity around Deal and Asbury Park. The Eighth Avenue "Flume," which runs with a will from Deal Lake in Asbury Park every time it rains, doles out a steady diet of trapped herring (alewives) that were hatched out the previous spring. To mention this here is not to tell anything that locals haven't known since their first cast. Once you get to the north end of Long Branch, the jetties drop off in quality—eroded, low, and short.

Bait writes the book on methods. April alewife runs have sharpies using them alive, if they can get and keep them. The potential for that doesn't end until late June. Come July, eels (both alive and rigged) come into play. A strong local flair for the use of rigged eels can be seen in the application of tin squids that are sewn into the eel's head. While lending enhanced castabililty, the squid gives the bait a better swim than God ever intended. During slow periods some like to use live calico crabs. As it is statewide, the September mullet run triggers a feeding binge that throws otherwise cagey and selective stripers off their guard. Metal (called "tin" farther north, regardless of true composition) comes into play, as do Rebels, Red-fins, Bombers, and Mambo Minnow swimmers. By fall (at these latitudes well into December) it is anything and anytime. Naturally, local surfcasters will accept some blues and weakfish as targets of opportunity, but, in this hard-core, highly esoteric subculture of surfmen, there is only one thing in life with meaning: a striped bass big enough to make a big man sweat.

CONTACT TIP: There is good surf information at Steven's Bait and Tackle, (908) 229–4954.

15

Sandy Hook Point
Sandy Hook, New Jersey

BEST MONTHS TO FISH: April through December.
RECOMMENDED METHODS: Drifting baits or plugs.

FISH YOU CAN EXPECT TO CATCH: Stripers, bluefish, and weakfish.

HOW TO GET THERE: Take Route 36 east from the Garden State Parkway. At Highlands follow signs north for Sandy Hook. End of the line is Fort Hancock. You can also follow the coastal road (Route 36) from Long Branch.

This northernmost location is a sandy spit dipping into the opening of Raritan Bay. The length of the Sandy Hook peninsula is 5 miles, which is no small reach into open water. One of the few openings *not* guarded by a jetty, the Hook is sandy shore that

Sandy Hook is Jersey's hot spot of hot spots with plenty of wading. Don't get run over by a Raritan Bay vessel.

reaches well into the bay, forcing fishermen to wade considerable distances. With night fishing most often the drill here, it is wise to carry a compass in case of fog and also watch for passing vessels that will often throw enough of a wake to fill your waders. Have an abiding respect for currents; while they make the fishing what it is here, they pose some risk to the overzealous surfcaster. This is known as a scary spot for good reason.

The Hook dips below the surface 3 miles north of the last designated parking area at Fort Hancock. At the ranger station on the way in, officials issue free parking passes for night fishing and ticket you if you don't have one. As buggies are not allowed, this is a spot for surfmen young enough to hoof the 6-mile round trip with enough left in them for fishing. Even the guys who clap their hands between push-ups won't drag a suitable fish back over these distances. Usually they bring along a scale and camera in a backpack to prove that the expected really happened. And it often does.

Nobody can be certain, but one explanation for the Hook being what it is, particularly in late fall, is that it serves as host to returning Hudson River stripers—a population, of late, that has never seen better numbers; if Chesapeake fish come there as well, it is doubly productive. This cowboy country is not quite worth the effort in summer, but certainly in spring and late fall it could be your best chance at a moose of a striper. Pack everything tight and light, using live eels and big plugs.

While the currents at the end are best, you can locate fish all along the way. Outside of bathing seasons, the Sandy Hook shore adjacent to the parking lots is more popular because of size and accessibility.

CONTACT TIP: Call Giglio's Bait and Tackle, (908) 741–0480, for Sandy Hook reports.

NEW YORK

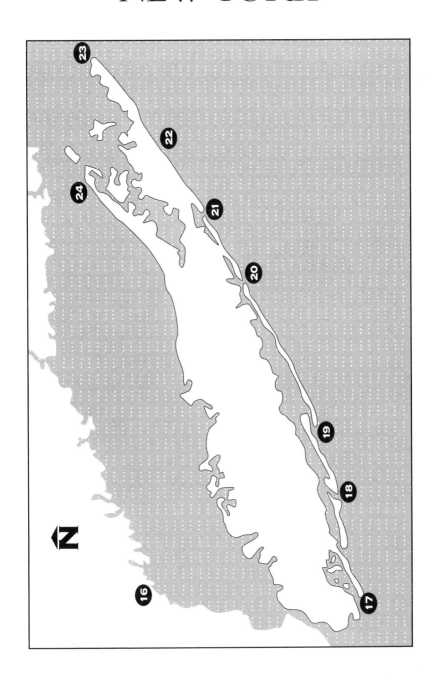

No doubt the greatest concentration of rabid surfcasters on the planet is in New York City. Their presence in an urban environment of that size indicates that opportunities for practice of their craft have got to be pretty bountiful. Along with all the traditional surrounding locations enumerated here, New Yorkers enjoy an astounding level of opportunity for shore fishing right in the city itself. Indeed, in the deep of night, great numbers and sizes of linesides are lured into the shadows of well-lighted docks, where sharpies who know how to find them succeed with impunity. The many bridges that lace the city offer similar, if not equal, opportunities. And yet, to enumerate small, dangerous, limited, illegal fishing spots would be both in bad taste and counter to the mission of this book. I raise my glass to those who dare risk a mugging, a towing, or territorial disputes in the name of striper fishing, though I need not follow in their footsteps.

In my tour of Cape Cod surfcasting that began some thirty years ago, I had the pleasure of befriending any number of New Yorkers with whom I shared many mid-watch hunts for striped bass. I found these surfmen to be aggressive because of where they came from; I found them hardworking because of an ethic that then had been instilled in them; and, lastly, I found them dedicated because of an all-abiding love for both the high surf and the greatest gamefish of modern times.

Sad to say, Long Island is cursed with both overdevelopment and a hoity-toity population that demands privacy and asserts its territorial rights well beyond the borders of its own property—an injustice not at all uncommon elsewhere on the Striper Coast. Therefore, in keeping with my mission here, I have not sought to disclose spots that are not reasonably accessible to outsiders. After all, we must never forget that we are all outsiders at some time or other.

16

Troy Dam
Hudson River
Troy, New York

BEST MONTHS TO FISH: Late April through early July.

RECOMMENDED METHODS: Alewives, big jigs, and swimming and surface plugs.

FISH YOU CAN EXPECT TO CATCH: Stripers, white shad, and small-mouth bass.

HOW TO GET THERE: From I–90 in downtown Albany, take 787 north for just under 6 miles to a traffic light. Take a right turn to Green Island on Tibbits Avenue. A couple of blocks on the left is an old Ford plant parking lot where anglers park, then walk down the bank.

Current, well-aerated powerhouse outflow, and both ground and live alewives to chum fish in are the key ingredients to this first Hudson River barrier. Anglers gather at this west bank location every spring to cash in on this curious set of both natural and man-made conditions. Fish with 20- or even 30-pound test lines to deal with the combination of crowds, current, and sometimes big fish to forty pounds.

Regulars watch for a 50-degree water temperature that occurs in late April while coinciding with the alewife run. Then fishers line the shore and toss live or freshly dead alewives upcurrent, letting the bait drift naturally in the white water under the powerhouse. Another favorite is to cast big swimmers, which simulate local baits. There is a very special top water action with surface plugs in June. Also, drift deep with oversize jigs with twister tails as an effective way to efficiently probe the depths in this current.

The most popular tides are on the moons, but avoid fishing during low water because the shallows make stripers spooky. Though fish can be taken around the clock, the best time is dark early morning; this is both a universal witching hour and a means of avoiding the mob. While fishers can score all summer and fall, those times are a mere shadow of spring's whoppertunities.

There is everything here including sturgeon, smallmouth, pike, carp, perch, and shad, which of late have been improving their run. Fish these with 6-pound mono tied directly to a dead-drifted shad dart.

CONTACT TIP: For an up-to-date rundown on what is happening at Troy Dam, call Tom at River Basin Sport Shop in Catskill, (518) 943–2111.

17

Breezy Point
Rockaway, New York, New York

BEST MONTHS TO FISH: October and November.

RECOMMENDED METHODS: Swimming plugs.

FISH YOU CAN EXPECT TO CATCH: Stripers, bluefish, and weakfish.

HOW TO GET THERE: Take the Belt Parkway East to Flatbush Avenue, then head south over Marine Parkway Bridge. Coming off the bridge, take the first left and follow signs to Fort Tilden for a National Park Service parking permit.

The Breezy Point jetty is one of the more reliable and accessible spots in the New York City area. Moreover, my contacts claim it, reluctantly, as one of the more underrated, underfished spots on the

Striper Coast. Be aware, however, that the jetty is a dangerous spot because of the slick stones. It gets "real snotty" with strong winds out of any of the southern quadrants, blowing pushy water over the top. For that reason, wear corkers or cleats to improve your footing, because even rescue doesn't like going out there. But slick rocks are a price that regulars are more than willing to pay for a steady dole of Moby linesides available there, particularly during fall months.

The tip of the jetty is best, because it provides access to the strong currents that develop there on either tide. A favored method is to fish big swimming plugs in the deep of night, but avoid teasers or droppers, as the current presses them against leaders, rendering them less effective. Old-time traditional New York swimmers like Danny's, Atoms—the big stuff—are what works here, I am told. Bucktails with pork-rind are also popular. Unique to this prominent Rockaway opening is that the current most often flows seaward, regardless of tide, because rising water backeddies. Thus, it is possible to feed a plug into the current to gain added distance in fishing coverage. Winds that support the natural movement of the water are most popular: southeast on the incoming at the tip of the jetty. During northeast and northwest winds, the sides of the jetty produce all through the incoming.

After the bathing season ends in September, a buggy can be a great help here. Also, four-wheelers with the appropriate permit (available at the Fort Tilden office) from Gateway National Seashore can run the beach out to the Breezy Point jetty at the west end.

Increasing numbers of surfcasters are recognizing that the beach area between the park service office and the jetty is highly productive in the fall, and the later the better. Not all surfcasters, however, care for mountain goating their way over slick rock piles. Expect good daytime action in the fall.

CONTACT TIP: Woodcleft Fishing Station, (516) 378–8748, in Freeport can report on the Breezy Point action.

18

Jones Inlet (West End 2)
Jones Beach, New York

BEST MONTHS TO FISH: October and November.

RECOMMENDED METHODS: Swimming plugs.

FISH YOU CAN EXPECT TO CATCH: Stripers, bluefish, and weakfish.

HOW TO GET THERE: Take Southern State Parkway to Meadowbrook Parkway south to signs for the West End 2 parking lot. Inlet is to the west.

While it is something of a walk out to the Jones Inlet jetty, it provides a flatter, easier set of stones to walk on and use as a fishing platform. The popular time is the last three hours of the outgoing tide at night. Best fishing is on the east side of the breakwater and in a pocket alongside the jetty. While plugs are popular, bait fishing produces as well. There is some bait fishing along the Jones Beach sand in summer, but look for big fish early October to late November.

In order to park here, a night fishing pass is required, with the only legal purpose being to fish.

TIP: When jetty fishing, have a length of rope with a hasp on the end to put through the gills of a big fish. Never try to climb out of a slick jetty carrying a Moby striper.

19

Fire Island National Seashore
Fire Island, New York

BEST MONTHS TO FISH: October and November.

RECOMMENDED METHODS: Swimming plugs and sea worms or chunks.

FISH YOU CAN EXPECT TO CATCH: Stripers, bluefish, and weakfish.

HOW TO GET THERE: East on Long Island Expressway (495), then south on the William Floyd Parkway to Fire Island. Also watch for signs to Robert Moses State Park.

The Fire Island Inlet is not as popular as those nearer to the city. The inlet itself is no longer guarded by a jetty on the south side and is sand. Short of the inlet, there is a rinky-dink little jetty of no real importance.

The best aspect of this area is the drivable 8 miles to which the buggy-equipped surf fisher gains access. Two jurisdictions are involved here—Robert Moses State Park and Gateway National Seashore—and both require beach permits. The Gateway permit is free, but rules regarding beach use vary too much from year to year to justify enumeration here. And while there is a fee for Moses, the permit can be used in other state areas, like the one at Montauk. Remember, if you drive out to Fire Island Inlet's south side with a buggy, park above the high-water mark, as there have been a number of vehicles flooded here. Driving the waterline in the fall, when stripers and blues are migrating, is a favored way to spot schools of fish. At night, regulars will stop periodically to test the water with a plug.

While the best of Fire Island is the inlet, which is approached from the south side, don't overlook the beach on the north side, which your south-side oversand vehicle permit entitles you access to in the fall. The north bank of Fire Island Inlet is just a continuation of Jones Beach. Sore Thumb and Gilgo Beach are watched closely by area mechanized surfcasters, and they can be fished by car from Ocean Parkway.

TIP: Never miss slack tide at an inlet because that is when the fish change position.

20

Moriches Inlet

Center Moriches, Long Island, New York

BEST MONTHS TO FISH: May through November, but fall is best.

RECOMMENDED METHODS: Swimming plugs, chunks, and fly fishing.

FISH YOU CAN EXPECT TO CATCH: Stripers, bluefish, and weakfish.

HOW TO GET THERE: Either from Route 495 or the Sunrise Expressway (Route 27), take the Shirley exit and follow the signs to William Floyd Park. (Oversand vehicle recommended.)

There is similarity between all the South Shore inlets in that the currents and jetties that guard them are the main draw and their reason for inclusion here. Like the other jetty-flanked inlets, you have to be part mountain goat. For Moriches, the most popular tide is the last two hours up and the first two down. Many diehards, however, will fish the drop all the way down. The main article in the inlet itself is swimming plugs at night, but just about everything is used during the good fall fishing found here. During summer, people will bait fish along the edges of the current with chunks. It is also possible to walk the back pond from the inlet to listen for feeding linesides in the deep of night. Such protected backwaters are perfect for fly fishing.

The safest and shortest approach is from the west, where it is possible to reach the jetty on foot. If you want to approach the inlet from the east, you can get a county permit for a buggy from any Suffolk County park. Washouts are common there and change the hazards of driving all the time; thus, from year to year it's hard to predict what you are going to run into in your efforts to approach the east jetty. As with most of Long Island's South Shore, full beach driving privileges begin September 15, but the serious migratory activity of gamesters coming down the beach will not begin until late October, when it builds with each passing day.

TIP: Fly fishers often ask if striper fishing is a case of pattern or presentation. It's presentation.

21
Shinnecock Inlet
Hampton Bays, Long Island, New York

BEST MONTHS TO FISH: May through November.

RECOMMENDED METHODS: Plugs.

FISH YOU CAN EXPECT TO CATCH: Stripers and bluefish.

HOW TO GET THERE: Take the Hampton Bays exit off Route 27 for the west side; cross the Ponquogue Bridge to the dune road and go left to the old Coast Guard Station. The east side is approached by oversand vehicle from Southampton (county beach permit required).

The west jetty that guards this fast-water inlet is easiest to approach and is popular during southeast and northwest winds. No offroad vehicle is necessary. The east-side hot spot—where you need a buggy—is a place at the jetty's end called the "Jungle." The word around here is that northwest winds move the current closer and that east winds help the casting: it is another one of those debates that rage about fishing and its more popular places. At this writing, the east jetty is being rebuilt. Common to both sides is the value of dropping water, particularly in the fall, but that is not to say that there is not some good fishing in the off-season and during the rising tide. Indeed, there is a lot to be said for avoiding crowds around here, even at the expense of missing the season's peak.

Once this far east, a frequent saying is that one might as well "mush on to Montauk," that great bastion of Long Island privacy.

CONTACT TIP: Call Richie Altenkirch, (516) 728–4110, for the inlet lowdown.

22

Nepeague Beach
Montauk, New York

BEST MONTHS TO FISH: September through November.
RECOMMENDED METHODS: Plugs and lures.
FISH YOU CAN EXPECT TO CATCH: Stripers and bluefish.
HOW TO GET THERE: Go west along the beach from Montauk. (Oversand vehicle recommended.)

Nepeague Beach lies west of Montauk, running from Heather Hills to the Montauk town line, a distance of almost 5 miles. Although this rocky stretch suffers a great deal of erosion, sometimes causing drivers to leave the shore to circumvent impassable areas, it does offer a chance to cover a stretch of shoreline adjacent to Montauk during the migration season.

According to locals, lures are by far the most popular method. Because it is a shallow area, best fishing is on the incoming tide; north winds, from the back, are most popular because they add distance to the cast. Driving is prohibited between 10:00 A.M. and

The best Nepeague fishing is in the fall on the night tides.

6:00 P.M. during the summer, but after September 15, this beach is open around the clock (with proper permit, available from the East Hampton Town Hall). This spot is kid sister to Montauk Point.

TIP: When reading a beach for the first time, see it at low tide.

23

Montauk Point
Montauk, New York

BEST MONTHS TO FISH: May through December, but fall is best.

RECOMMENDED METHODS: Plugs and lures.

FISH YOU CAN EXPECT TO CATCH: Stripers, bluefish, weakfish, blackfish, and fluke.

HOW TO GET THERE: Go east on Route 27 to land's end in Montauk. (Oversand vehicle is optional.)

Any time you take on the job of writing about a place like Montauk, the problem becomes one of perspective: Just limiting yourself to the hot spots within the hot spot becomes a challenge. The surf fishing at Montauk could be a book in itself. Thus, in the name of brevity, I will limit myself to those observations that will be of the most service.

Montauk Point is a place where the currents of a hundred sources converge. Depending on wind and tide, the water can be moving in any given direction, gathering and sweeping bait as it goes. And in addition to being an usually productive place to fish, it is eminently well known. Consequently, Montauk's curse is that it is the prime fishing spot for New York City surfcasters—no small following—who are all after the glamor species. Moreover, it is highly accessible to the foot traveler, which only contributes to the crowding.

Generally speaking, the north side—North Bar and False Bar—is favored during north winds. East winds, if they are light enough, tend to move currents and bait in, which improves the fishing, but once an east wind picks up to around 15 knots, water can become

Accessible and public, Montauk is one of the Striper Coast's best fishing areas.

weedy and silty, making things impossible—a common intensity-dependent situation. Worth mentioning is the fact that a heavy rain will cause clay along the shore to discolor the water enough to shut fishing down. Tide preferences vary with the many locations spread around the curve, and even then are reliant upon wind. This is one of the few places in the world where you will find surfcasters fishing in wet suits, particularly on False Bar and North Bar. On foot, there are as many proponents of the south side of the light. It is a case of how far a surfcaster is willing to walk. Don't overlook both Rocky and Culloden points on the north side, a few miles short of Montauk Light. One informant told me that many is the occasion that the real job was being done there while others were skunking out at Montauk proper.

Naturally, an oversand vehicle extends one's angling radius, enhancing the opportunity to avoid crowds. Three jurisdictions are involved in issuing beach permits: the state handles the lighthouse area; Suffolk County handles Shagwong; and Ditch Planes issues town permits. The requirements (four-wheel drive and the usual jack, shovel, board, tire gauge, and tow rope) are the same for all three.

Just as you are apt to see anybody and everybody fishing, you'll find all methods in use, from drifting live pogies carried by elaborate bait wells to chunks of frozen ones. From bucktails to poppers, if it has ever worked for stripers and blues, you'll see it at Montauk. Some generalizations that work everywhere: poppers and tin by day; swimmers by night. Whatever Montauk is—and it is a mecca for fanatical surfcasters—it is a multiple of itself in the fall. Just how early the insanity begins, or how late in December it ends, is the wild card. Never take a top-rated hot spot lightly!

CONTACT TIP: Johnny's Bait, (516) 668–2940, knows the Montauk ropes.

24

Orient Point
Greenport, New York

BEST MONTHS TO FISH: May through December, but fall is best.
RECOMMENDED METHODS: Plugs and lures.
FISH YOU CAN EXPECT TO CATCH: Stripers, bluefish, and blackfish.
HOW TO GET THERE: Go east on Route 25 (Soundview Avenue) and follow the signs.

The tip of this Long Island north-fork peninsula offers shore fishing opportunities similar to those at Montauk. It is a bit rockier and more protected but less crowded. Thanks to a surprisingly large area of state land, access is among the best on the Island. From Horton Point, on the west, all the way around the tip of Orient to the ferry slip is a good 13 miles. While you can't fish it all, there are ten or twelve pull-offs along the road where you can go down to the water and fish ¼ mile or more on either side. Truman Beach is a popular spot, as is the shore between the gut and the ferry landing (the southeast corner), but the opportunities can vary with time, tide, and wind to create potential for them all. Onshore north and nor'west winds are okay so long as they are not two-flaggers. Oddly enough, the spot that ought to be hot, Plum Gut, has little to offer the surfcaster. It seems that the really working water is out of reach, making this a boat fishing hot spot. Keep Orient Point in mind if a severe east storm or southern quadrant winds huff up and spoil the rest of Long Island. There is protection here and options that can keep you fishing when others are playing canasta behind shuttered windows elsewhere.

Plug fishing holds the greatest fascination here but, once summer bluefishing starts, there is interest in chunking the bottom. Of course, like everywhere worth listing, the target species is stripers, but keep in mind that Orient Point may be the best blackfish (tautog) place on the entire island, with two great runs at each end of the season—May and October—and it ain't exactly shabby in between. Use sea worms in spring and little green crabs in fall. Split the big ones with your knife before baiting up. The season lingers here, according to my spies, right up until Christmas.

CONTACT TIP: For Orient Point fishing information, call A.P. White, (516) 477–0008.

Orient Point offers varied fishing and is the coast's best blackfish fishing area.

CONNECTICUT

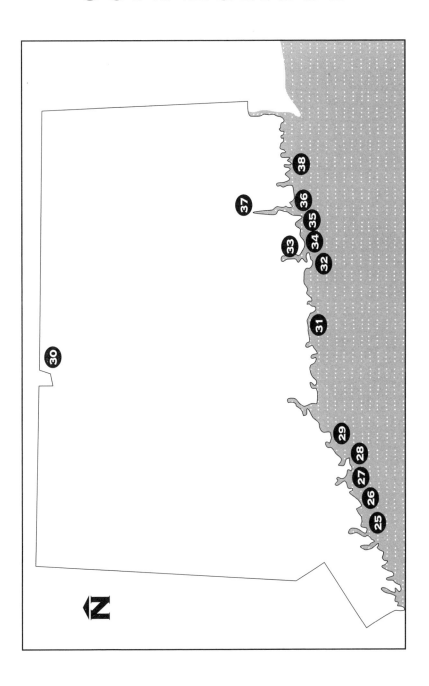

Private ownership of the shoreline reduces Connecticut's attractiveness as a shore fishing location. Indeed, nearly all the spots listed here are within the bounds of state parks. No doubt there is excellent fishing in any number of other places, but local private control prevents access through a complicated variety of ordinances, selectively enforced parking regulations, and illegally hidden rights-of-way. Thus, and this is by no means unique to Connecticut, access opportunities are better for nearby residents, who enjoy circumvention and immunity. Usually, when our sweethearts wish us luck, they're referring to the fishing; for Connecticut they mean the parking.

Having said this, I am, nevertheless, pleased to report that the public property that emerges from my research is well chosen. A more dispassionate critic would probably regard the spots I've listed for Connecticut as exemplars of "multiple use," but I can't shake the feeling that they were either chosen by a fisherman or chosen with fishing uppermost in mind. Good fishing is no small criterion for the siting of state parks in this state. Modern policies, which will influence access in the future, favor a more reasonable balance in utilization of coastal resources. Today, waterfront sites have to provide meaningful public access, and the shore-bound angler can look forward to greater access opportunities as a result.

Unique to this chapter is the fact that government input was greater here than in any other state. First, Ron Rozsa, a biologist for Long Island Sound Programs and an enthusiastic shore fisherman as well as striperman, read some of the copy during its preparation and directed me to an even better source in Rod Macleod, a biologist for Connecticut Marine Fisheries. With Macleod's input I had so many hot spots that the cuts list was nearly as long as the list of places I've described—not because Connecticut is superior, but because my information for this state was so complete and derived in such measure from professional sources. It's what these guys do.

Another anomaly that I bumped into, much to my delight, is that this state is awash with saltwater fly fishers. Thus, while it is not the case, the notion that Connecticut's fly fishing is better than elsewhere emerges here, more as a result of local insistence than natural conditions.

What fun fishing you could have going to the places that have *failed* to make the cut. I commend the following to your indulgence with the reminder that all the judgments in this book are ultimately subjective:

Greenwich Point Park, Stamford
Shippan Point, Stamford
Sherwood Island State Park, Westport
Pleasure Beach/Town Pier, Bridgeport
Long Beach, Stratford/Bridgeport
Stratford Point, Stratford
Power Plant on the Housatonic, Devon
Milford Harbor East and West Jetties
Sandy Point, West Haven
Noank Town Dock
Rocky Neck State Park, Old Lyme
Black Hall River Bridge

25

Calf Pasture Point and Town Pier
South Norwalk, Connecticut

BEST MONTHS TO FISH: March through June, and September through November.

RECOMMENDED METHODS: Chunks, plugs, fly fishing, and sea worms.

FISH YOU CAN EXPECT TO CATCH: Stripers, bluefish, winter flounder, and some blackfish.

HOW TO GET THERE: Take exit 16 off I–95 and turn left at the traffic light onto East Avenue. Follow East Avenue to traffic circle, then bear right onto Gregory Boulevard. Take a right onto Ludlow Parkway and follow it to its end.

People who fish the town pier like to use cut bait (chunks) of menhaden, herring, or mackerel held on the bottom with a sinker. The popularity of this spot would preclude any opportunity for lure fishing during all but the deepest hours of the night. Best tide phase at this spot is high water, when it is not possible to fish the bar out front. The pier is also popular in September for snapper blues when they are at a point in their development of inch-per-week growth. Look for some decent winter flounder fishing in March with sea worms. There is some blackfish fishing, but that is not what has made this spot.

On the bar out front, the gang enjoys plugging swimmers like Rebels, Mambo Minnows, and Red-fins tied direct. Wading is not possible until the tide is down to around halfway. If the fishing proves to be any good, regulars will stay until rising water forces them off;

the drop, because of combining currents of the Norwalk River, has an edge. Protected by the Norwalk Islands, the bar is popular with fly fishermen. As with the pier, if there is room and water is low enough for a sand spike, some people will chunk from the bar.

John Baldino, fishing from a boat in the Norwalk Islands right off Calf Pasture Point, landed a 71-pound striper only a few years ago. This proves that the big mamas can be there.

During daylight, a town parking permit is required between Memorial Day and Labor Day, but fishing is open to anyone after closing time. There are fewer hassles in spring and fall.

CONTACT TIP: Call Fisherman's World, (203) 866–1075, for Calf Pasture Point information.

26

Cedar Point and Compo Beach
Westport, Connecticut

BEST MONTHS TO FISH: March through June, and September through November.

RECOMMENDED METHODS: Swimming plugs, cut baits, sea worms, and fly fishing.

FISH YOU CAN EXPECT TO CATCH: Stripers, bluefish, and winter flounder.

HOW TO GET THERE: From exit 18 off I–95, get onto the Sherwood Island State Park Connector northbound, then take a left (west) onto Green Farms Road. A left onto Hills Point Road leads to the beach. Take a right (south) onto Compo Road, then take the next left for the entrance.

These two spots are combined because they are adjacent and fished and spoken of by locals in the same breath. Cedar Point is a little more protected at the river mouth, while Compo Beach is more open to the Sound. Opportunities here reflect those at Calf Point. Differences often develop around the type and location of baitfish that have drawn gamefish here in the first place. It is a case of who has the bait where the bunkers happen to be. Naturally, the influence of the Saugatuck River at the west end (Cedar Point) holds an

Crowded by day, western Sound areas offer good fishing for school stripers in the deep night.

edge for the dropping tide, but the open water and stony shore of Slates, on the east end of Compo, more than compensate for that.

Depending on the winds, the fly fishers prefer the river mouth, and so much the better if the tide is dropping. There is enough space here for you to fish bait or plug, with some anglers doing both—plugging with their eye on a baited rod. At the west end of Compo Beach, in front of the cannons, there is a serious blackfish run spring and fall. Tackle shops say to block out early May and late October on your calendar.

As at Calf Pasture, summer hassles and parking stickers are the rule, but the best fishing is at the two quiet ends of the season. While there may not be any 70-pounders on the record books for this hot spot, all agree it rates one better than Calf Pasture.

CONTACT TIP: Call the Sportsman's Den, (203) 869–3234, for more on Cedar Point and Calf Pasture.

27

Penfield Reef

Fairfield, Connecticut

BEST MONTHS TO FISH: May through November.

RECOMMENDED METHODS: Fly fishing and swimming plugs.

FISH YOU CAN EXPECT TO CATCH: Stripers and bluefish.

HOW TO GET THERE: Take exit 22 from I–95 to Round Hill Road to Route 1; then take a right. At the traffic light, take a left onto Reef Road, which leads to the Sound. Parking is available at a recreation park on the left side. Across the road, on the left, about 50 yards past the stop sign, there is a walkway between two houses, which, after ¼ mile, leads to a beach walkway.

Penfield Reef is a rock-and-cobble sand spit that extends into Long Island Sound for about a mile. During low tide, the spit is exposed enough for fishermen in waders to follow it down. Thus, this place is popular during a falling tide. One of the few spots where fly fishing leads the way, it remains a good place for plug fishermen who utilize swimming plugs during the night.

Of course, the above rules are not hard and fast. Cut baits can be used—tackle shops say that live eels are becoming increasingly popular, and no doubt there are other species available at selected locations. Those who know their way around here in the dark of night do use the flood tide to their advantage, but until you know the ropes, I would not advise you to chance getting confused in a rising tide and getting trapped in deep water.

TIP: If flies are no good for stripers, then why do plug fishers use them as teasers or droppers?

28

Saint Mary's Beach, Ash Creek, and Henry J. Moore Fishing Pier
Fairfield, Connecticut

BEST MONTHS TO FISH: April through November.

RECOMMENDED METHODS: Cut bait (menhaden, herring, or mackerel) and swimming plugs.

FISH YOU CAN EXPECT TO CATCH: Stripers, bluefish, blackfish, and fluke.

HOW TO GET THERE: Ash Creek and the Moore Fishing Pier are at the South Benson Marina. From I–95 take exit 23 to Route 1 south. Take a left (after McDonald's) onto South Benson Road, then a left onto Oil Field Road, then a right onto Turney Road to the marina. For Saint Mary's Beach, take exit 25 off I–95 onto Fairfield Avenue south. Take a left at Gillman Street and continue to the east side of Ash Creek. Parking and access are provided.

Saint Mary's Beach faces the open Long Island Sound where the bottom is composed of boulders and rocks. Across from the beach is the Henry J. Moore Fishing Pier, which is actually an extension of a rip-rap embankment bordering Ash Creek Channel. The channel is popular with stripermen who watch the creek at night for feeding linesides that gorge on bait there, particularly during a falling tide. Menhaden schools frequent Ash Creek and are often trapped in the marina basin by predators. Blues exhibit the same behavior as stripers but are more likely than stripers to do so in daylight. For day anglers, there is a good fluke run in the channel out front during the late summer and early fall. The rocky bottom of Saint Mary's appeals to blackfish in spring, when their spawning run is on. Look for them the third week in April and use sea worms. Many wanted to rate this spot a three for stripers—a tough call.

CONTACT TIP: St. Mary's Beach, Ash Creek information is available at Ted's (203) 366–7615.

29

Silver Sands State Park (Charles Island)
Milford, Connecticut

BEST MONTHS TO FISH: May through November.

RECOMMENDED METHODS: Fly fishing, swimming plugs, and cut baits.

FISH YOU CAN EXPECT TO CATCH: Stripers and bluefish.

HOW TO GET THERE: From I–95, take exit 35, Schoolhouse Road south. Turn right onto Route 1 (Bridgeport Avenue), then left onto Meadows End Road. Follow Meadows End straight onto Pumpkin Delight Road. At the end of this road, turn right onto Monroe Street, then left onto Nettleton. Turn left at the barricade onto the park service road and follow it to the end. (Access will be changing, as this park is presently under development, and it still is unclear how roads will be managed.)

The major attraction of this hot spot is a ½-mile bar that connects with Charles Island. Wader-clad regulars like to work the rips that form between the island and shore, but access to the island is only possible at low tide, and it is necessary for anyone who goes there to keep in mind the potential for being trapped. Because surf fishing is best done at night, it is mandatory that anyone doing any wading here be certain about tide, visibility, and direction. Until you are completely familiar with the area, be especially cautious.

No doubt other species can be taken here, but the targets are stripers and blues, and artificials dominate the methods. Silver Sands is not for everybody. On the other hand, if you know the striper ropes, this is a place worthy of finely tuned attentions.

Swimming plugs tied direct—not encumbered with a wire leader—work well on slurping stripers. Fly fishermen should plan to use floating lines and the usual streamer patterns. Good spot.

CONTACT TIP: For more information on Silver Sands and other local spots, call Stratford Bait and Tackle, (203) 377–8091.

30
Enfield Dam
Connecticut River
Suffield, Connecticut

BEST MONTHS TO FISH: Late April to late June.

RECOMMENDED METHODS: Alewife baits and big swimming plugs.

FISH YOU CAN EXPECT TO CATCH: Stripers.

HOW TO GET THERE: From I–91 take exit 47B to Route 190 west. After crossing the river, take Route 159 south, then take the first left onto Canal Street.

Another herring run fishery that is highly seasonal, Enfield Dam reflects population trends of both indigenous bait and stripers. Each spring linesides follow alewives and white shad up from the Sound to the eroding dam where both mill about. Without bait there are no stripers.

While anglers line up on both banks to toss baits and plugs, the west bank has the edge because of two nearby holes, better flow characteristics, and the availability of parking at Old Canal Park. Dependent upon snow melt, spring water levels can be highly variable: One day fishermen can wade far out into the river among the rocks; another day the river roars white, nearly burying the dam.

With such conditions there is some hazard to the river. Drownings take place every year, for example, although most victims are from boats. While examining conditions, it is good to keep in mind that water temperatures, which trigger the runs of both bait and predators, are more suitable when the water is low because snow melt is colder. Otherwise, the later in the season, the better and bigger the bass run. As with the rest of the Striper Coast, small fish arrive first, more in April, and the cows become numerous in late May. Look for a top fish in the low forties and a predominance of smaller linesides. Naturally, the river will mirror coastwide population trends.

Amazingly similar to No. 16, Troy Dam, you may have to fish heavy tackle more to deal with the current and crowds. Locals can often be seen carrying two rods—a light 6-footer for snagging baits and a meat stick for the actual fishing. Here, a freshwater fishing license is required despite its tidewater status.

CONTACT TIP: To inquire about Enfield Dam, call Hartford Club Sports Center, (860) 296–0110.

31

Hammonasset Beach State Park
Madison, Connecticut

BEST MONTHS TO FISH: May through November.

RECOMMENDED METHODS: Sea worms, chunk baits (bunker and mackerel), live eels, poppers, and big swimmers.

FISH YOU CAN EXPECT TO CATCH: Stripers and bluefish.

HOW TO GET THERE: From I–95 take exit 62, then follow the signs to the park.

The rock jetty at Meigs Point attracts the majority of angling atten-

Stu Jones, who read Striper Surf, *holds a Meigs Point schoolie that he caught, "like garden worms for trout."*

tion within Hammonasset Beach State Park. Bottom fishermen tend to gather here in large crowds during seasonal peaks and weekends. (Fishing is limited to the jetty during the summer season.) The waters at the very end of the jetty are most popular because of the depth there. By fall, particularly after dark—a time when the best fishing of the year is available—this spot is pure solitude. The entire beach is open after Labor Day, and it is not uncommon for great schools of bluefish to be seen within casting distance. Park personnel issue permits for fishing after closing time so that anglers can drive their cars from the entrance gate to the beach.

Madison's Stu Jones, winner of the 1994 Massachusetts Governor's Cup with a 57-pounder, likes Meigs Point. "I like the flood better than the ebb here because of how the rip makes up with the jetty," said Jones. "During falling water your eel or plug has to go through rocks that are fouled with old tackle and lines that are caught there. But during the rise the current flow is northwest and the rip line sets up right at your feet. I flip eels underhand back at the submerged rocks, drifting them through the rip like garden worms for trout. I have been pretty successful."

CONTACT TIP: Antlers and Anglers, (860) 245–1007, can advise you on Meigs Point fishing.

32
Cornfield Point
Old Saybrook, Connecticut

BEST MONTHS TO FISH: May through November (but skip August).
RECOMMENDED METHODS: Plugs, eels, fly fishing, chunks, and crabs.

FISH YOU CAN EXPECT TO CATCH: Stripers, bluefish, and blackfish.

HOW TO GET THERE: From I–95 take exit 67 onto Route 1 south, take a left at the light onto Route 154 south, follow to a left turn onto Cornfield Point Road, and continue to land's end.

All of this rocky shoreline is productive, but the fishing improves as one makes one's way west to the point. Watch for evidence of moving water, which is more likely down to the right. Big swimming plugs are popular here as are live eels, but because of the rocks, eel retrieve speeds should be slightly faster to keep them from getting lost. Fly fishers like the sand flats to the north. You can also access these flats from the Old Saybrook Town Beach, although public access is often restricted in the summer.

As in any other southwest-facing location, winds from that quarter improve things; however, a strong southeaster, usually an indication of an impending storm, also makes the interaction of the currents better. Starting in early October, there is a great fall run of good-sized blackfish that take green or hermit crabs like candy.

This is a popular local spot with fragile access considerations. Some anglers park at the rear of the Castle Inn lot, but officials tell me that it is illegal to do so and that your car may be towed. Yes, parking is a problem.

CONTACT TIP: River's End Tackle, (860) 388–2283, knows Cornfield Point and more.

33

Connecticut Department of Environmental Protection Marine Headquarters
Old Lyme, Connecticut

BEST MONTHS TO FISH: March through December.

RECOMMENDED METHODS: Baits or lures, depending on the species, and fly fishing.

FISH YOU CAN EXPECT TO CATCH: Stripers, bluefish, winter flounder, and blackfish.

HOW TO GET THERE: Take exit 70 from I–95 to Route 156 north; then take a right onto Ferry Road and continue to land's end. There will be signs.

A new fishing pier, completed in the spring of '93, extends from the south end of the state property (beneath the Old Lyme railroad bridge) to the mouth of the Lieutenant River—a fly-fishing mecca. This one earns hot-spot status because it is highly accessible and productive on account of its placement on the Connecticut River—hardly a risky call. Open twenty-four hours a day, it is intended to be the answer to the problems that so often bedevil shore fishing. Fly fishers leave the end of the pier and wade the bars in the deep night with floating lines. Patterns are dressed to imitate river shiners, sperling and—some years—baby bunker.

CONTACT TIP: Information for this area and other spots is available from River's End Tackle, (860) 388–2283.

34
Sound View Beach
Old Lyme, Connecticut

BEST MONTHS TO FISH: May, June, October, and November.

RECOMMENDED METHODS: Plugs, live or rigged eels, and fly fishing.

FISH YOU CAN EXPECT TO CATCH: Stripers and blues.

HOW TO GET THERE: From I–95 take exit 71 onto Four Mile River Road. Take a right on Route 156 at the stop sign, then a left onto Hartford Avenue and follow to the end. Parking is limited and at your own risk.

Two major areas of structure on this sandy, gently sloping beach should be tested first. About 300 yards west of the parking lot, there is a small rocky point that is popular two hours either side of high tide. Outside those hours, efforts should be cursory, and I'm told that the sand before that is a waste of time.

The other spot, Griswold Point, is about a mile west and just about as far as many of us are willing to walk. Matt Zajac, however, tells me that it is Connecticut's answer to the Cape's old-time Chatham Inlet, only smaller—and well worth the effort. The reason for this is that currents from the Blackhall and Connecticut rivers collide with Long Island Sound to create a garland of moving water, bait, stripers, and blues. Here, juvenile herring and menhaden emigrate from the nearby Connecticut River in late summer and fall (mature spawning baitfish earlier). Onshore sou'west winds stir it up for better fishing, and nor'westers cause the Connecticut River water to move better. Casting from shore, you can reach a depth of 13 feet. There is excellent fishing all through the dropping tide here, so try it after having worked the aforementioned rocky outcropping at high tide. While all methods work, this is dreamland for fly fishers. Possibly the best-in-state!

Information central for this region is River's End Tackle (860–388–2283), across the river in Old Saybrook, where Pat Abate knows what is happening and where, as well as what you'll need.

CONTACT TIP: North Cove Outfitters, (860) 388–6585, knows Sound View Beach.

35

Niantic River
Niantic, Connecticut

BEST MONTHS TO FISH: May through November.

RECOMMENDED METHODS: Bunkers, herring, bucktail jigs, live eels, and fly fishing.

FISH YOU CAN EXPECT TO CATCH: Stripers and bluefish.

HOW TO GET THERE: For the western shore, take exit 74 from I–95, to Route 161 toward Niantic, then make a left at the light onto Route 156. Either take the left road before the Niantic River Drawbridge and follow to the end, or take a left immediately after the drawbridge, then a left at the stop sign. Safe parking on the west, or Niantic, side of the river is limited to the access ramp on the north side of the road. Eastern shore access is from Route 156, Rope Ferry Road; at the traffic light, turn north onto Niantic River Road, take the first left onto B Street, turn left onto Fourth Street, and take the first right onto Rope Ferry Road to public parking at the end.

Fishing is done from the railroad bridge at the mouth of the Niantic River. To the south, or seaward of the railroad track, you can fish both sides of the river. There is also good fishing on the west bank between the bridges. Beaches on both sides of the river mouth produce good fishing, with the eastern shore having an edge.

Water flies under the railroad bridge on the Niantic River, so use heavy tackle and be ready for Mr. Big.

When there are bunker in the river—and thus the opportunity to snag fresh baits—it is possible to feed one from this bridge and do very well with both stripers and blues. At times, there have been some Moby blues taken here in this way. Currents from this river bridge are too powerful for bottom fishing, and plugging, except at slack tide, is not a viable alternative. But a bucktail jig, for those who use them well and allow them to drift deep, can be used for stripers in the night if there are no fresh baits available. Best water is during the drop in tide. Pat Abate, a local regular with a coastwide reputation, told me that about twenty years ago there was a striper taken here that weighed in the mid-sixties. Not too shabby. Eddies or slack tides in which you can hold bottom produce some decent blackfish. It is possible to fish bottom on the south side of the inlet. Also, some surfcasters like to fish live eels by casting and retrieving slowly.

Just about any bait found coastwide is represented here and thus can be used with delivery methods dictated by the motion of the water. Anglers have been known to lament the oft-repeated complaint that bass will show up in the Niantic—usually in the deep of night—slashing and slurping but not taking any baits or artificials. Abate says that this happens when the squid are abundant, but it may also occur during June worm hatches, which have driven otherwise calm people stark raving mad. South of the inlet, particularly on the outgoing tide, when bait is being swept past, the action can be better than in the inlet. That is one reason why it is a popular fly-fishing spot.

CONTACT TIP: Hillyers Tackle Shop, (860) 443–7615, knows what is happening on the Niantic River.

36

Harkness Memorial State Park
Waterford, Connecticut

BEST MONTHS TO FISH: May through November, though August is slow.

RECOMMENDED METHODS: Plugs, cut baits, eels, hermit crabs, and fly fishing.

FISH YOU CAN EXPECT TO CATCH: Stripers, bluefish, blackfish, and some fluke.

HOW TO GET THERE: From I–95, take exit 75 toward New London. Make a right at the light onto Route 213 and follow to the park entrance.

Best fishing is west (to the right) of this rocky, curving shoreline. The boulder-strewn shore offers plenty of attractive hiding places for good sized stripers. There is also a reef within casting distance that no doubt draws some linesides to the area.

Some Harkness regulars will come equipped to fish cut bait (menhaden or mackerel) but have a supply of plugs in the bag— swimmers at night and poppers by day—for when they see or hear fish working. Of course, when things are known to be good, surf fishers will come with live eels. While stripers are what most are seeking, bluefish often end up as targets of opportunity. With all the rocks, this is also a great blackfish spot starting in early October. Use green or hermit crabs with a bank sinker on the bottom. The sandy shallow areas near Goshen Cove are popular with fly fishers who use floating lines.

Best fishing time for all methods is two hours either side of high tide, particularly when this period matches up with dawn or dusk. No parking hassles.

TIP: When night fishing, slow your retrieve if you can see phosphorescent plankton in the surf.

37

Thames River
Norwich, Connecticut

BEST MONTHS TO FISH: December through March for winterovers; April through November for migrant stripers and bluefish.

RECOMMENDED METHODS: Sea worms, eels, bucktails, plastic worms, and selected plugs.

FISH YOU CAN EXPECT TO CATCH: Stripers, winter flounder, and bluefish.

HOW TO GET THERE: From Route 395 north, take exit 79, left onto Route 163 at the stop sign, then right onto Powerhouse Road. Park on the right at the railroad tracks. The Montville Power Plant is located off Route 32 in Montville on the west bank of the Thames River.

The Thames River is unique in that it is one of only two winter fisheries among the listings in this book. This river enjoys a moderate migratory population of stripers that winter over. In late winter, usually the last week in February, seasonal temperatures and warming waters from a nearby power plant get resident bass feeding. Thus, locals are fishing for stripers here at a time when there is virtually zero activity on the rest of the Striper Coast.

The Montville Power Plant's warm water outflow packs in

schools of stripers during the springtime. Small swimmers, Kastmasters, Fjord spoons, Rattle Traps, and bucktail jigs are productive. Tide has no meaning here; it is a case in which the warm water discharge *must be flowing* in order to attract fish to the area. Using light tackle, anglers commonly catch and release dozens of fish.

Best spot is on the west bank, south of the power plant. Regulars gather here to fish blood worms, once they are available; until then, many shore fishermen like to use eels on a 5/0 or 6/0 hook held on the bottom with a bank sinker. The plug fisherman's choice is a small Mirr-o-lure or a rigged plastic worm. Expect rare stripers up to about 30 pounds, but the average is more like 5 pounds. While a few linesides remain well into April or May, fishing is so good elsewhere by then that there are few anglers left to see them off.

With a valid freshwater license, it is legal to fish here all winter, but the striper season is closed from December 15 to March 31. Regulars utilize this fishery on a catch-and-release basis, which is how most bass fishing is now practiced all along the coast. Naturally, winter flounder—targets of opportunity because of their table value—are a welcome by-catch.

The above suggests that the Thames is somehow deprived of traditional seasonal angling opportunities just because it has a winter fishery. Hardly. There is a great run of linesides in spring—after the season for taking begins—which is thought to be drawn by the robust schools of spawning herring (alewives); this bait sustains activity well into June. Fort Shantock State Park, in Montville (off Route 32, north of Pequot Bridge), is famous for the success anglers have using its live herring on the big bass that arrive fresh and hungry.

Even the Norwich marina and dock, right in town, produce with herring. Those who don't have live baits still do well with hook baits of menhaden and mackerel chunks in addition to swimming lures and bucktail jigs. Authorities say that the flood tide is best in Norwich and that bluefish can be caught in the harbor from June through October because the bunker go there every summer.

Gales Ferry (take Route 12 to Stoddard Wharf Road), according to the Division of Marine Fisheries, is a famous summer hot spot with a three-star rating for stripers and skillions of bluefish. Here the river makes a bend and the main channel comes within casting range from the riverbank. While menhaden are the forage base, chunks, swimmers, and surface poppers also do the job. A couple of final points: first, by consensus, winter fishing is rated four, the rest of the year three; and second, if somebody tells you that the Thames is a winter-only place, he's trying to snowball you.

CONTACT TIP: Ken's Tackle Shop, (860) 445–6888, is up to date on Thames' fishing.

38

Bluff Point State Park
Groton, Connecticut

BEST MONTHS TO FISH: April through November.

RECOMMENDED METHODS: Plugs or baits, depending on the species.

FISH YOU CAN EXPECT TO CATCH: Stripers, bluefish, blackfish, scup, and winter flounder.

HOW TO GET THERE: Take exit 88 from I–95 to Route 117 toward Groton. Take a right on Route 1, then a left at the traffic light onto Depot Road, and follow it to the end under the railroad tracks and into the park.

The rocky shoreline at Bluff Point is about ¾ mile from the parking lot. Striperwise, things don't get going here until June, but they hold well into November; expect blues from July into November. All the methods—cut baits and plugs—that work elsewhere are utilized here. Among the rockier areas, expect some blackfish (tautog) in late April. The best bait then is a sea worm on the bottom with a bank sinker. For scup (porgies), fish the sandy areas with freshwater-sized light tackle using a fingernail-sized sliver of squid or a small section of broken sea worm with a trout hook. The first scup appear in June, and they become more numerous as summer goes on.

Poquonock Cove, which is off to the west in the park, and closer, is a good spot for winter flounder in early spring on the flood tide. Use sea worms and the same small hooks.

CONTACT TIP: Fish Connection, (860) 885–1739, will tell you about Bluff Point Fishing.

Bluff Point offers some good light tackle fishing for all species.

RHODE ISLAND

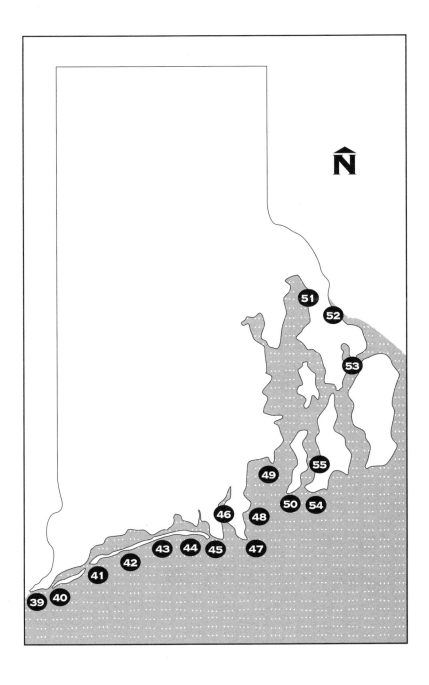

It might sound great on paper to read that this little state has a 400-mile coastline, but that is another one of those nook-and-cranny measurements. The truth is that the Ocean State can be divided into two sections: the south shore beaches (about 20 miles), and the area related to Narragansett Bay. The beaches are pristine, and the waters off Narragansett and Newport, both rock-bound shorelines without comparison for natural beauty, are said to be so clear that they are favored by divers. Sad to say, deep into Narragansett Bay, the water is severely polluted. Still, gamefish are not deterred from going inland, clear to Providence, and the bay affords some protection from sea storms.

Coastal policies are favorable to fishing, and Rhode Islanders love the natural opportunities the sea provides. Still, as has been the case in areas to the south, there is some overpossessive behavior, a lot of it (but not all) from visitors. As elsewhere, there have been battles over beach access, and courts have ruled that a landowner's control ends at "mean high tide." Among Rhode Island's ever-lengthening list of scandals, there has been an expensive rights-of-way study that showed that people abutting such rights-of-way have long hidden them with a little ivy, stone, and mortar to cover and hide the public's access to the shore. Worse, signs that were meant to inform the public have repeatedly been taken down to prevent encouragement of their use. But my home state's failings seem worse because I am familiar with them, not because people here abuse the public's right of access more than elsewhere. We who love a place are often the harshest critics.

Still, it is a good place to fish, in that it affords the shore fisherman a hundred times the opportunity of any place this side of New York. It is the beginning of access opportunities that have been sorely missed since mid–New Jersey. I can say this with some comfort when examining those spots that failed to make the cut.

At this writing, the old Jamestown Bridge (take Route 138 to Jamestown) is projected for development as a fishing pier. In the past, I have taken any number of 40-pounders from it—with trailer trucks passing so close that their backdraft pulled at my jacket.

Local residents, however, have already organized objections to having "rowdy" fishermen there. If we are not tossed out, it will be a great place for porgy and summer flounder by day, stripers and blues by night.

A little over a mile north of the Jamestown Bridge is Rome Point Inlet. This opening to an estuarine pond behind Hamilton Beach is a popular spot for local light tackle anglers, and one-handed surf rods and fly-fishing tackle predominate here. Evening high tides, which are always moon tides, are popular because of the hour, as the best fishing takes place in the evening when there is less intrusion upon a person's sleep, which is no small consideration when surfcasters are choosing between fishing and making a living.

Upper Narragansett Bay has a number of locally popular spots that have their nights. Sandy Point, Conimicut Point, Warwick Light—to name but a few—yield stripers in spring and bluefish on summer nights when menhaden are available; yet it would be a violation of my mission if I were to elaborate any further upon them: not because they are secrets, but because they are of only local significance. Barrington Beach fell short by the whisker of a midge.

39

Napatree Point
Westerly, Rhode Island

BEST MONTHS TO FISH: May, June, October, and November.

RECOMMENDED METHODS: Plugging, live eels, and fly fishing.

FISH YOU CAN EXPECT TO CATCH: Stripers, bluefish, fluke, porgies, and bonito.

HOW TO GET THERE: From Westerly, take Route 1A south; then pick up Watch Hill Road at Avondale. Take a right into the parking lot at land's end.

Guarding the east edge of the opening to Little Narragansett Bay, Napatree Point is a 1¼-mile barrier beach of generally sandy shore that ends in a rocky point. While you can find bass or blues anywhere along this stretch, the rocky point is the most reliable spot on account of the rips that form here and on offshore reefs. Where the sand meets the rocks is a good location during the ebbing tide, which flows right to left. On this seaward side, wind from any southern quadrant will cause the surf to collide with currents if the tide is dropping. On the incoming tide, fish any of the rocky shoreline to the right. When the tide is rising, the wind can combine with these currents to form a better rip. Don't overlook the eddy on the inside edge in the back. "The Naps" are a popular fly-fishing spot, particularly on a north-side mussel bar. The walk out is an invigorating ramble in the majesty of a Rhode Island sunset.

I omit the summer months from this hot-spot listing because of parking problems. During the bathing season, night access is difficult and day access just about impossible.

CONTACT TIP: From Watch Hill to Quonnie, call Captain Don's Bait and Tackle, (401) 322–0310, for fishing information.

40

Watch Hill
Westerly, Rhode Island

BEST MONTHS TO FISH: October and November.

RECOMMENDED METHODS: Plugging.

FISH YOU CAN EXPECT TO CATCH: Stripers and bluefish.

HOW TO GET THERE: From Westerly, take Route 1A south, then pick up Watch Hill Road at Avondale. Follow the signs to Watch Hill Light.

Watch Hill Light, a Coast Guard station, has limited parking facilities that are restricted to authorized vehicles. It is best, therefore, to park in the lot at Watch Hill across from the carousel and walk the quarter mile out. This rocky peninsula is a natural obstruction for passing gamefish, which have to go around it. A natural spot for plugging, with its open water surf, Watch Hill Light is usually fished at the crack of dawn or at sunset. It is especially popular during the fall migration. Traditionally, the best side is the east, a rocky place where casters often position themselves on a prominent stone, risking getting dumped off by a pushy sea. Like all coastal stones, they can also be slippery.

Those with an oversand vehicle can access the light from the east by driving the 2 miles of beach that are open during the fall. Entry is gained from Misquamicut. At the corner, where the sand beach meets the rocks of the light, I have seen stripers and blues packed in during a raging, prestorm southeast wind, when the surf was white with foam and the only thing breaking the coloration was the green and dark backs of stripers and blues. I hasten to add that the 2-mile stretch of beach itself can provide angling opportunities for both lure and bait anglers, as the bottom here is sandy and free of obstruction. In some years, the outer bar structure here is as good as that of Misquamicut, to the east. Incidentally, do not try to

The beach east of Watch Hill Light entertains Moby blues and bass.

fish in front of private property at Misquamicut Beach during the summer.

CONTACT TIP: Information is available from Watch Hill Flyfishing, (401) 596–1914.

41

Weekapaug Breachway
Westerly, Rhode Island

BEST MONTHS TO FISH: October and November.

RECOMMENDED METHODS: Plugging and fly fishing.

FISH YOU CAN EXPECT TO CATCH: Stripers and bluefish.

HOW TO GET THERE: Follow signs from Shore Road (Route 1A) south to Weekapaug, or turn south on Dunn's Corner Road.

Winnapaug Pond is a natural estuary that provides a haven and breeding ground for baitfish that appeal to stripers. There is a constant flow that fills and drains this pond through the opening of Weekapaug Breachway, which is flanked by a pair of rocky jetties. During a dropping tide, you can see the lines of infusion as currents of the estuary reach seaward. Naturally, the shallow waters of the pond are heated by day, and in autumn they are cooled at night. No doubt these variations in temperature, along with the scent of bait, exert some influence over passing gamefish. As a result, the opening at the end of the two jetties is a popular spot for surfcasters. A good method is to drift live eels seaward with the current. That is easy here because of the smooth, sandy bottom. Moreover, with a road bridge only a few hundred yards upstream, one can park on either side to fish from whichever jetty suits one's fancy.

CONTACT TIP: Weekapaug Bait and Tackle, (401) 322–8058, can tell you what's happening here.

42

Quonochontaug Breachway
Charlestown, Rhode Island

BEST MONTHS TO FISH: May through November.

RECOMMENDED METHODS: Plugging, jigs, live eels, and fly fishing.

FISH YOU CAN EXPECT TO CATCH: Stripers, bluefish, and occasional bonito.

HOW TO GET THERE: For the west bank: follow the shore road east from Weekapaug. The oversand route is private, but the Rhode Island Mobile Sports (RIMS) fishermen honor members of other beach buggy associations. Nights or off-season, you can park at the beginning behind the dunes and walk the beach for good fishing. For the east bank: Just east of the intersection of Route 216 and Route 1, take a south turn onto West Beach Road and follow it around a circle to the west until it ends at a public boat-launching ramp.

"Quonnie," as it is so fondly known by regulars, is the first of a number of classic striper hot spots that deserve special treatment. I say this because this hot spot has its own legion of rabid followers who will no doubt be wretching in the dunes when they see their

favorite spot in these pages. And the reason is: Quonnie has everything.

The breachway, which is an inlet flanked by jetties, leads to a
clean back-pond estuary. Moreover, the passage to Quonochontaug
Pond is both short enough and straight enough to permit an exchange of water of sufficient force to keep the inlet from silting
over or slowing down. The key to this spot is the power of these
tidal exchanges, because during the drop, Quonnie Pond water
reaches far to seaward, rolling in forage and gamefish. My guess is
that the gallonage here is double that of the aforementioned
Weekapaug Breachway.

Of course, these dropping currents produce the top striper fishing opportunities in the region. At the seaward end of the jetties,
surf fishers cast across current, then free spool swimming plugs seaward until their spools are depleted. Then they let their plugs swing
under tension through the flow and pause in the eddy, following

Quonnie is a surfcaster's paradise—rated four for good reason.

with a slow retrieve. Works easy. At the early part of the first outward flow, many surfcasters will fish the east jetty; however, this is not a good spot once the tide is down some, because the shallows of that bank often cause plugs to hang up on rocks. Moreover, I have seen some good fish lost in these rocks. Access is from West Beach Road, off Route 1. Use your head parking and keep in mind that local cottage owners notice less in the deep of night and in the off-season.

The west bank is the best side for drifting a plug in the dropping tide. Access, however, presents certain challenges—and this is no accident. First, it is 1½ miles down the beach, which is best covered with a four-wheeler; second, no beach driving is allowed in Rhode Island without a Coastal Resources Management Beach Permit issued at nearby Burlingame State Park on the north side of Route 1 in Charlestown; third, this is a private, residents-only beach. What can work either for or against you is that RIMS members are counted as landowners there. This means that each member has access rights to Quonnie, and they are permitted to have guests. Thus, if you can take the right people to dinner, barter some choice tin squids, or offer help at some other time and territory, you just might be able to fish there. Membership in United Mobile Sportsfishermen is honored. And there are other ways.

The same road you would use for the east bank (West Beach Road) also leads to state land in the back where the breachway opens to the pond. Here you'll find a public boat-launching ramp and free parking with virtually no restrictions except for camping. It is an easy matter to cross with a float tube, canoe, or other marginal craft, and after a short walk to the front (less than half a mile), it is possible to fish from state property without trespassing.

A great deal is made of the seaward end of Quonnie Breachway on the dropping tide. It is one of those local traditions that is pretty hard to dispute. You can't argue with all that history. Also, there is a certain esoteric group of hard-core regulars who dearly love meeting on the rocks to drift plugs, gab, knock down a beer or two, and otherwise celebrate the glory of surfcasting.

The rise in tide, particularly if fish have been showing on the drop, can compensate for a slight loss of bass with a great increase in solitude. Five fish that are all yours are better than a hundred shared with thirty other casters. With water coming in—hurrying to the back pond with the will of seamen on liberty—it is possible to drift heavy bucktail jigs all through the opening. Landing, however, is the problem. Even big fish, after fighting the current when heading to the open sea, will eventually drop back into the breachway. To land them, you will have to deal with the rocky banks. Unlike your counterpart fishing the dropping tide who can beach a monster, you will have to climb down slippery rocks amid often vicious currents.

But now for Quonnie's easier part: in the back, where the jetties end and the back estuary begins, it is possible to drive the family auto (as mentioned earlier) to the east side. Here, walking north on the flats in waders, a shore fisherman can enjoy the quiet, protected, estuarine nature of Quonnie Pond. It is a perfect spot for light spinning tackle with smaller plugs. Or, where better to fly fish than among shallows, where sperling skitter across the surface while pursued by hungry linesides? No police hassles, no crowds; your worst disturbance is likely to be teenage "parkers" who might not understand the importance of discreet headlights. Also, never overlook the breachway itself, as you will often find some Moby linesides hanging out in the currents there. If the quiet and deep night mood of the back has one failing, it is that it can lull you into a false sense of comfort, so that you will not be ready when Mr. Big comes along. It happens all the time.

TIP: For greater backing capacity, take advantage of the new, Kevlarish braids that offer today's 60-pound test at half the diameter of yesterday's 50-pound lines. Technology.

43

East Beach
Charlestown, Rhode Island

BEST MONTHS TO FISH: June through November.

RECOMMENDED METHODS: Plugging, live eels, and bottom baits.

FISH YOU CAN EXPECT TO CATCH: Stripers, bluefish, blackfish, weakfish, flounder, and porgy.

HOW TO GET THERE: Access is south from Route 1 on East Beach Road, the first right after the fire station. (Oversand vehicle recommended.)

I have a love/hate relationship with East Beach. On the "hate" side: deep water and invisible structure make it a poor spot for the practice of reading the beach. Every yard of this shore, and I have fished every one, feels no different than any other. Two notable exceptions are "The Mound," roughly 3 miles east of the beach access, where there is an ocean current, and a stretch west of the breachway where you can sometimes feel cobblestones on the bottom. I have felt them many times, but only after a diver told me about them. Also, about 200 yards to the west of the breachway lies "Split Rock"—a pair of rocks usually at casting distance—which has ocean current flowing by in which linesides sometimes hang out. Otherwise, it is a straight, lackluster beach with little for a beach reader to sink his or her teeth into. Now to the parts I love.

It is all sand—no wrecks or anything that will damage a line. The breachway's jetty acts as a stopping point where bait is often trapped. A similar situation occurs 4 miles to the west, at Fresh Pond Rocks. Stripers, and certainly blues, can be anywhere along the beach. Moreover, at the base of the angle of the beach, there is a place called "The Rut," where there is a small drop-off of 6 to 12 inches caused by the erosive action of the surf. I have hooked many Moby stripers so close to the beach—all hanging out at "The Rut"—that I could easily have lifted my eel out of the water before they took it.

I have also come upon schools of stripers while plugging or eel fishing. All methods work here, and I have seen anglers sitting on their tailgates in fall, watching lines baited with squid, chunks, or sea worms. The daylight panfishing here is about as good as it gets. It is possible to sweeten a hook with a tiny ribbon of squid or a ½-inch section of sea worm and feel drumming and tapping the whole time you are fishing—and filling a bucket with delectable 8-inch porgy. I have caught a variety of fish here, including blackfish, weakfish, flounder, and even kingfish. This assortment of fish that appear here in varying levels each July and August should remind us that all marine populations are highly cyclical. Weakfish, for example, at this point in their cycle, are not to be found except in limited numbers in the mid-Atlantic states. Summer flounder are in decline right now, and scup are all over the coast in numbers that make you feel that the bottom must be lined with them. I can recall times when, during the November migration, I inadvertently caught stripers, blues, weakfish, and cod on the same lures, although opportunities for cod from the beach are unreliable most years.

Naturally, the fall migration elevates the popularity of East Beach, particularly in early November. There have been few fall seasons when, driving the beach at night, stopping periodically along the way, I didn't find stripers, or blues, or both. One reason for the reliability of this spot is that oversand vehicles are permitted on the 4 miles of productive beach. The ability to drive the beach introduces an element of efficiency to one's efforts that is not possible elsewhere on this section of coast until you reach the Cape.

One note, though, concerning driving on East Beach: because this shore is one of those fragile ecosystems that hang in the balance and could be denied to surfcasters by the carelessness of just one driver, religious observance of the rules is necessary for the continued access of this fine stretch of shoreline. If the wheel of your vehicle kills so much as one tuft of beach grass, or a single plant of beach plums, you are finished with driving the beach—and the fines are severe. If it happens with any frequency, we are all finished! Stay on the trails. Stay off the dunes.

Two usage types are available, according to the season: front beach, for the period September 15 through April 15; and back trail, for the rest of the year. Keep in mind that all regulations are subject to change, and this book cannot serve as legal justification for any behavior. Any departure from where you are supposed to be at a given season, or from the regulations as they stand, is reason for revocation of the permit.

No doubt the rest of Rhode Island's south shore offers similar fishing opportunities, but utilization of a beach vehicle is not permitted on the stretch that includes Green Hill and parts of Matunuck. This gives East Beach an undeniable advantage.

TIP: To detect night-feeding stripers, look for a dark stain in the surf or listen to hear the fish splash and gulp.

44
Charlestown Breachway
Charlestown, Rhode Island

BEST MONTHS TO FISH: May through November.
RECOMMENDED METHODS: Plugs, bucktail jigs, live eels, and fly fishing.
FISH YOU CAN EXPECT TO CATCH: Stripers, bluefish, bonito, and blackfish.

HOW TO GET THERE: Follow the signs from Route 1 in Charlestown. There is a state-run parking area for anglers.

Five miles east of Quonnie, you'll find a geographically similar situation in Charlestown. The main difference is that access to both sides of the flanking jetties is through public property. On the east bank, the state maintains a "Public Fishing Area" with two parking

Charlestown Breachway's east jetty draws the crowds for good reason.

lots: One is for anglers' autos; the other is a self-contained area for camping vehicles. All east-bank access is on drivable road. The west jetty to Charlestown Breachway, on the other hand, is accessible by a 4-mile oversand trail that requires four-wheel drive and a permit and is closely regulated.

The inlet here provides slightly less flow than that of Quonnie despite the fact that it serves a much larger estuarine pond. This is because the channel to the inside is narrow, shallow, and winding. Worse, with reduced flow, siltation tends to accelerate the closing of the channel. About every twenty years, give or take, the government has to come in and dredge the channel out to keep the back pond alive. If you are unfortunate enough to try this area when the channel is in need of dredging, you might be disappointed with Charlestown Breachway's fishing because of subdued currents. At this writing, a cycle is about midway through.

As it is with Quonnie, drifting plugs on the outgoing tide is popular—only, in this case, it is the east jetty that enjoys the bulk of angling interest. There are three reasons for this: First, the east jetty is more accessible; second, during the falling tide, ocean currents moving east bend the seaward lines of infusion to an east hook that produces a favorable eddy; and, third, the regrettable bad positioning of "Plug Rock" on the west side makes the east jetty the clear choice. On either bank, however, there is deep water.

Placement of the stones and their later rearrangement by the forces of nature make the east jetty a lot wetter than the west. I have often stood on the west side on a night when the wind was heaving a murderous sea, and the east-side boys, walls of water raining down on them 20 feet back from the end, made you wish you could do something to relieve their suffering. Of course, being on the drier side was small compensation for the hazards of having Plug Rock, which is covered with barnacles that can nick a line down to half its rated strength, a scant 20 yards downtide. And yet, the west side is usually better during a rising tide. I have seen Moby linesides position themselves in the opening and around the end to face the current. Here it is possible to drift a live eel, plug the outside, or run a bucktail jig through the strongest currents. But again, I advise you to fight a fish that goes out *against* the current with all you can muster, because Plug Rock remains a hazard; it is the *big* fish that swim against the current when in trouble. I have paid their price. A common angling mistake here is to fish with gear that is too light.

A choice time to keep in mind is when the sea current changes to early rise while the breachway current is still falling; then, for about two hours, the hook, or eddy, will be on the west side, which favors that side. Another terrific period is slack tide, about three hours after high or low tide on the tide chart for this location, when all fish change positions for a better feeding opportunity. Tautog fishing—using little green crabs for bait—is easier at slack tide. Because this spot is flow dependent, moon tides (new and full) are best. If you happen to be around during a brisk southeast, that wind favors Charlestown for some reason. Keep in mind, however, that southeast is the wind that precedes storms.

The back of the breachway, all the way to the open back pond, can produce some surprisingly good fishing at times; however, boat traffic is heavy here and one would do best to explore in the deep of night during the week. Small fish are more likely here, but I really hesitate saying that, because the ocean is loaded with wild cards. Great fly fishing here.

CONTACT TIP: For information call Breachway Bait and Tackle, (401) 364–6407.

45

Deep Hole
Matunuck, Rhode Island

BEST MONTHS TO FISH: April, May, October, and November.
RECOMMENDED METHODS: Lures and fly fishing.
FISH YOU CAN EXPECT TO CATCH: Stripers, bluefish, and fluke.
HOW TO GET THERE: There are two accesses to this area: Deep Hole proper is approached from the south side of Route 1 on Matunuck Beach Road. For the east end of Matunuck go south, or right, from Route 1 by using Succotash Road from U.S. 1 to find East Matunuck State Beach and the West Wall.

The most dramatic alteration in the otherwise straight structure running east of Charlestown Breachway lies in Matunuck. Starting with Carpenter's Bar, which is so shallow that it is largely exposed at low tide, there are a number of worthwhile natural structures that appeal to stripers. Many striper regulars will gather at Carpenter's during the tail end of the drop and will endure, if there is any action, until rising water drives them off the bar. Carpenter's, by the way, is the spot where, according to local legend, the great author and surfcasting aficionado Jerry Sylvester suffered a fatal heart attack while fishing.

Just east of the bar is Deep Hole, where the bottom falls off green, and surf breaking over the left edge of the bar fades so quickly that any caster is reminded how easy it is to get into trouble. The hole is so large, so dramatic, that you are not going to miss it. Moreover, Carpenter's and Deep Hole are so close to one another, adjacent really, that most anglers rarely bother to distinguish between

Deep Hole Matunuck is a famous April and early May hot spot.

them. Deep Hole is a public fishing area with parking provided.

There is roughly a mile of beach between Deep Hole and the Matunuck West Wall. The eastern part of this is Matunuck State Beach, where there is ample parking. Access to that eastern section is from Succotash Road. The western portion, a stony, less inviting area for bathers, is a comfortable ramble on foot. All is legally accessible public property. The eastern border is the Harbor of Refuge guarded by a breakwater that reaches seaward for over ½ mile, which, season depending, is Matunuck's major contribution to local striper fishing.

Each spring, around the last week of April, the first school stripers make their appearance. These are the smallest, earliest migrants, and they come nowhere near keepable size with the regulations now in place. Schoolies as small as 12 inches, and rarely over 22, show up each season in astronomical numbers. I have seen dozens of surfmen lined up along the first 300 feet of jetty, facing west (the outside), each surf rod down hard with a thrashing schoolie. It is a traditional greeting place for first fish of the season and enjoys an uncommon reliability. The tradition of fishing there for stripers that small was established during a time when size limits were more liberal, when a keeper needed to be a mere 16 inches. Then, a large enough percentage of the fish that were caught were legal. But with the high fishing ethic that is observed today, I'm not sure if Matunuck's West Wall is any longer a viable fishing spot, as all fish at this time of year are throwbacks. I'm not sure it is good for the species to have so many people catching and releasing them with *some* mortality. This period of small fish is only a little over two weeks, followed quickly by larger bass and a few prespawning blues that will disappear quickly to some offshore spawning ground until summer. Look for fluke or summer flounder on the inside of the wall from July on. Years ago, when cod were available in greater numbers, I caught them there all winter with skimmer clams on the bottom, and March was the best month. No more.

TIP: Popping bugs will often draw followers that don't take, so watch for swirls and put on a streamer.

46
Harbor of Refuge
South Kingston, Rhode Island

BEST MONTHS TO FISH: May through November.

RECOMMENDED METHODS: Lures, live baits, and fly fishing.

FISH YOU CAN EXPECT TO CATCH: Stripers, bluefish, fluke, and pollock.

HOW TO GET THERE: For the west side, use Succotash Road from Route 1. For the east bank, take Route 1 to Route 108 south, then right on Galilee Road.

Salt Pond, as the Harbor of Refuge is sometimes called, is a major tidal estuary that reaches 5 miles inland. It is guarded by the West Wall (discussed in number 43) and the East Wall, at Point Judith; there is also a center wall with openings at each end that constrict water to produce substantial currents. Much of the harbor is shallow with only a small navigable channel for the sportfishing boats and the commercial fishing fleet that are moored there. These shallows, however, provide fertile opportunities for any number of forage species, which appeal to stripers throughout the season. For instance, there is an alewife run in spring; sea worms (*nereis*) are hatched out in June; and I have seen schools of bunker and tinker mackerel: Mars bars and Twinkies if you are a striped bass. While it is a famous spot for boat fishing in the deep of night when other traffic tends to be subdued, it can still be moderately productive for shore fishing.

Naturally, the greatest currents are at the narrowest places, which occur where the jetties meet the shore. It is possible to fish either bank, but the best access is on the east, or Galilee, side, near a restaurant called George's, which is famous for shore dinners. Here you'll find a short jetty where you can plug, jig, or drift bait in currents on either tide. I would not advise bottom fishing here because of currents that will push a sinker to shore too quickly. Just ⅒ mile into the estuary from the docks that service the commercial fishing fleet, the widening of the channel and milder motion of the tide permit a bait and sinker to hold nicely. In this area, gurry is tossed over, or dispersed, from the fish houses, drawing baitfish and hungry stripers. For many years there has been a small group of hard-cores who quietly spirited out some Moby linesides that would have made anybody's day. Of course, with the height of the dock above the water, it is necessary to have a long-handled gaff and very heavy lines—40-pound test or more—to keep such big fish from winding their way and your line among the crustaceans of the dock pilings. Squid is popular.

Along the swampy shore of the west side, it is possible to wade a couple of hundred feet toward the channel and lay a cast of chunk bait on the bottom, then free spool it to a sand spike and wait for Mr. Big to come along and eat it. A wise flycaster can wade these flats with a streamer, listening for the slurp of feeding bass. Both tides produce, but all my action on this Jerusalem side has been on the rise. The west side of the Harbor of Refuge is found at the far end of Matunuck's Succotash Road.

Back on the east side, if you take a right at the end of Galilee Road, you will come to the Great Island Bridge, which crosses a narrow opening that connects with a secondary tidal pond. Currents under this bridge are powerful, the area is well lighted, and the shadows underneath the bridge are a great spot for linesides to lie in ambush for baitfish. Once, during a night when I had gone to a number of places in search of stripers with no luck, I went there only to come upon the dark figure of a fish lurking in the shadow. Tossing my bucktail jig upstream in anticipation of where the current would take it, I watched it disappear in the maw of a decent fish of around 20 pounds. After a vicious tug of war, I beached it upcurrent. Then, fishing blind because I could no longer see any fish, I felt the take of four more stripers of comparable size! To this day, I can never fish the Harbor of Refuge or even drive through the town of Narragansett without keeping that spot honest.

For years there was an annual pollock run in late April when anglers gathered to take them in great numbers at sunset inside the harbor. If this species ever returns to the numbers of the past, this will be the spot to watch at this early time.

TIP: The worm hatch of late spring can put so much bait in the water that fishing can be frustrating. Don't panic.

47
Point Judith
Narragansett, Rhode Island

BEST MONTHS TO FISH: June through November.
RECOMMENDED METHODS: Plugs and lures, and some bait.
FISH YOU CAN EXPECT TO CATCH: Stripers, bluefish, porgy, and flounder.
HOW TO GET THERE: From Route 1, take Route 108 south to Point Judith.

One glance at the map will tell you that Point Judith juts prominently out into open water and that moving gamefish are likely to pass close to shore. This shallow stretch of rocky coast lies in the foreground of a Coast Guard station. With ample parking outside the gate, military authorities have never closed off access to the spot in the thirty-five years that I've known of it. One of those rare instances in which tradition has it that the best striper fishing is with popping plugs by day, low tide seems to have an edge by allowing casters to wade closer to a sea current that passes the lighthouse. To the right of the lighthouse foreground, facing open water, there is a drop-off, or hole, where the foam breaks over nearby bars, then fades with the new-found depth of the hole. It is a great place for a plug to be washed into—swimmers in the night, poppers during the day—as gamefish often gather there. A southeast wind would favor such a situation.

Some surfcasters also like to bait this hole with a chunk of menhaden or other traditional striper bait. Don't try this, however, if someone is plugging it or is already there with bait, as he or she is most likely having success with another choice of bait.

Camp Cronin

To the right of Point Judith, you'll see a breakwater that is sometimes called the East Wall; this is the other flanking jetty to the Harbor of Refuge (hot spot number 44). This undeveloped state park has spacious parking in full view of the jetty. The jetty is popular during the fall migration of stripers and bluefish. Both ends hold promise for deep night probing of the shoreline: the far end, because it has a current developed from the waters of the harbor, and at the shore, where the jetty meets land. It should be pointed out that the latter is often filled with a collection of weed that makes fishing impossible, but winds can change that.

The East Wall is also a popular spot in summer for day fishing porgy and flounder.

TIP: When using a teaser or dropper, leave enough space between it and the plug for a good-size fish to fit between them without having its flanks scratched by the plug.

48

Narragansett's Rocky Shore
Narragansett, Rhode Island

BEST MONTHS TO FISH: October and November.

RECOMMENDED METHODS: Lure casting.

FISH YOU CAN EXPECT TO CATCH: Stripers, bluefish, and occasional bonito.

HOW TO GET THERE: From Route 1, take Kingston Road or South Pier Road onto Ocean Road, Narragansett.

The rocky shore of Narragansett is a series of striper hot spots that begin at Point Judith and continue northeast into the mouth of Narragansett Bay.

With the exception of Scarborough State Beach, there is little sand here until the town seawall, 5 miles up the coast at the pier; still, the nooks and crannies of stone to the east of the state beach, beginning with Black Point, are popular spots. From then on, the ragged shoreline offers ample hiding places for forage species. Most stripers—fewer big fish during summer and larger numbers in autumn—are taken surprisingly close to the rocks. This brings us to a number of tactical considerations not yet covered in earlier pages.

Surfcasting along these rocky shorelines requires the angler to select a suitable landing spot *before* beginning to fish. Otherwise, the hooking of a large striper could turn out to be a disastrous experience. Most of the shore here is high enough above the water to make reaching down quite difficult, if not impossible. You'll need a long-handled gaff and a spot with lighter surf that's close enough to the water for gaffing. Otherwise, all successes will be confined to mediocre fish. But most noteworthy are the hazards unique to this kind of shoreline. It is very easy to trip on the rugged stones, and at the waterline, where black algae grows on the rocks, the footing is nearly always as slippery as ice. To make matters worse, once in the water, it is often impossible for a person to get out—and the sea will batter a person against the rocks, causing injuries that can easily lead to drowning. It is often observed here that your best bet in a moderate sea is to swim seaward in hope of being picked up. Thus, the conditions described above combine with the popularity of this area to make Narragansett the number-one killer of surfcasters on the Striper Coast, and this dubious distinction is earned over and over again, every season. Back to fishing.

Tradition dictates that fall is the best season here for stripers and

The Narragansett rocks can be wet and nasty, but the fishing is good.

blues, and daybreak the best time. Little attention is paid to the tide, and I know of no rule here that considers it. East and south-east winds—in the face—make fishing impossible. In October, commercial fish traps are put up with running lines set out from the Newton and Hazard Avenue shores. These lead migrating fish seaward, justifying the popular notion that few will be along the shore on the southwest sides of the net. As a result, people tend to fish on the left side of the net runners.

CONTACT TIP: Narragansett, Narrow River, and Harbor of Refuge questions can be answered by Quaker Lane Bait and Tackle, (401) 294–9642.

49

Narrow River Inlet
Narragansett, Rhode Island

BEST MONTHS TO FISH: June through November.
RECOMMENDED METHODS: Plugs, live eels, and fly fishing.
FISH YOU CAN EXPECT TO CATCH: Stripers and bluefish.
HOW TO GET THERE: Walk east, or left, along the town beach from Narragansett.

Since we are still in Narragansett, it is necessary to distinguish be-tween Narrow River and the rest of town, because there is so much to be said for this important section of seascape. This is, of course, another of those fertile estuaries that are loaded with the bait and foraging opportunities that our linesides so love.

When you look east from town—from what is known as Narragansett Pier, where the seawall ends and the town beach begins—the inlet is the last thing you see before the rocky shore starts up again. It can be approached by walking the beach from town or, if the guards at the gate of the exclusive Dunes Club are feeling charitable, by parking in the lot—after which you still have to walk east to the inlet. The southwest shore of the inlet is all sand, the opening guarded on this side by a series of bars before the bottom drops off to a deeper channel. In full view on the far bank, and slightly seaward, is a garage-size stone called River Rock.

Local anglers like to take advantage of a dropping tide, fishing from the shallow bars and casting into the river's currents. Casts are made toward River Rock, then allowed to swing across the current to the eddy on the near side. Even with the tide way down, it is possible to free spool some line for a more distant drift.

As is so often the case, this is another one of those places where good fishing can be available on the incoming if linesides are lined up and panting on the outgoing. With currents sweeping around the point in the beach and hurrying to a rise on the inside, a beautiful rip forms where it is possible for a swimming plug to work itself into a frenzy or you can drift an eel upriver. Timing for this alternate approach is high tide. Any time flood occurs in the evening, say, 7:00 to 10:00 in this location, and it will be a moon tide (new or full). Consequently, the amount of water exchanged will be maximized. This is all-hold-your-rod fishing, a case of casting artificials as opposed to baiting and spiking a rod. This is also a great spot for fly fishing.

A couple of years ago, one early November night, I had some fresh pogies (menhaden) that I chunked and put on the bottom a couple of hundred yards short of the inlet so that sinkers wouldn't be swept by the tidal currents. Fishing with a pair of rods, hits from huge bluefish (14 to 16 pounds) were so fast and furious that I had to retire a rod and hold the one that remained.

An alternate approach to Narrow River Inlet is from the other bank—take the first right after Sprague Bridge when going north on Route 1A. While this is a public road, there are no parking signs, and local residents—this does change with the seasons—usually call the police. There is also a small public lot at Sprague Bridge where it is possible to launch a canoe for the short paddle downstream. If you can get there, fishing from River Rock sometimes has an edge over the sandy side.

Every autumn, there is a run of hickory shad, and late winter brings a run of white perch that are caught in the headwaters a few miles upstream. Narrow River Inlet failed to earn a rating of four largely because of the difficulty of access, but it can sometimes provide some top-rate fishing.

TIP: The salmon angler's riffle hitch—a tie that runs from the throat of the fly—causes the fly to leave a V-shape wake on the surface that gets attention.

50

Conanicut Island (Beavertail)
Jamestown, Rhode Island

BEST MONTHS TO FISH: July through November.

RECOMMENDED METHODS: Plugs.

FISH YOU CAN EXPECT TO CATCH: Stripers, bluefish, bonito, and albacore.

HOW TO GET THERE: Traveling west on Route 138, make a right (south) onto Beavertail Road, which is the first traffic light after Jamestown Bridge; then you'll go a little over 2 miles to Beavertail Road. From the east, take a left after crossing the Newport Bridge, then a right onto Narragansett Avenue, which leads south to Beavertail Road and land's end at the lighthouse.

On Jamestown (Conanicut Island), Beavertail Light is a classic striper spot with all the rocky shore hazards mentioned in the Narragansett section. This is a state park without parking fees, permits, or related governmental hassles. It is here that the old-time striper charters used to work the shore against a forbidding sea to cast swimming plugs toward the rocky shoreline. It is just as good from shore. Use swimming plugs at night for big bass; switch to poppers at early morning and during daylight. Fish right in front of the lighthouse, but don't hesitate to work the shoreline in either direction, especially if there's a touch of the mountain goat in your blood. Naturally, although this is a classic, well-known striper hot spot, expect bluefish as well as late-season bonito and albacore.

The entire south shore of Conanicut Island, from the tail east 5 miles to fort Wetherill, is loaded with striper nooks and crannies. Both Hull and mackerel coves are known for providing a continuation of the striper opportunity found at Beavertail. Some years, during the fall migration, bass will roam the sandy beach on the north edge of Mackerel Cove. Look for the cove on your left on the way out to the tail.

CONTACT TIP: Greg, at Creek Bait, (401) 423–1170, knows the island.

51
Barrington River
Barrington, Rhode Island

BEST MONTHS TO FISH: May and June.
RECOMMENDED METHODS: Alewives, plugs, and fly fishing.

FISH YOU CAN EXPECT TO CATCH: Stripers.

HOW TO GET THERE: From I–195 in East Providence, take Route 114 south into Barrington. The water on your left is the Barrington River.

Emptying into the northeast corner of Narragansett Bay, the Barrington River illustrates the importance of estuarine rivers to the overall well-being of striped bass. During the lean spring season, when little forage is available along the coast, linesides tend to congregate in hot spots like this one to cash in on the feeding there. Grass shrimp, sperling, numerous species of mummichugs, and sea worms compose part of these forage opportunities, but the main draw is the many small stream runs of alewives that begin in April and expel spent fish until mid-June. Then, in fall, the young of the season's alewives are dropping down to touch off another feeding bonanza.

Needless to say, a striper hot spot is not made by feeding opportunities alone. With no industry or concentrated development along the immediate shore, eel grass thrives, and water quality, when compared to similar parts of the coast, is surprisingly high. While some opportunity remains here throughout the bass season (May to November), the alewife runs are what make this river what it is. Schoolie fishing begins the first week in May and larger fish, 20 to 30 pounds, follow a few weeks later. Contrary to the popular belief that alewives are followed closely by stripers, it is the *spent* fish—the easy ones to catch—that the Moby linesides are looking to cash in on, and these are not available until late May or early June.

The Barrington tends to get more fishing pressure than its counterpart, the Warren, because of accessibility, what with roads along most shorelines. The Massasoit Avenue Bridge, near the white church off Route 114, is sometimes used. Upriver (north of the church), One Hundred Acre Cove, a grassy marsh in plain view from Route 114, harbors good numbers of small fish in some early seasons. Just above Barrington, from the northbound lane of the Wampanoag Trail, you will see a nature walk that leads to a point that guards the more open parts of One Hundred Acre Cove. There is a nice tide rip here on the mid-incoming for light tackle, particularly for fly fishing. South on Route 114 about 2 miles, behind the Barrington police station, it is possible to drift bait in the river from an old railroad bridge that is now used as a bike path. In early June, the regulars there can be seen in the deep night nodding over rods that trail alewives in the current.

TIP: You can add dramatic distances to your fly casting by using a shooting head.

52

Warren River
Warren, Rhode Island

BEST MONTHS TO FISH: May and June.

RECOMMENDED METHODS: Alewives, sea worms, plugs, and fly fishing.

FISH YOU CAN EXPECT TO CATCH: Stripers and white perch.

HOW TO GET THERE: From I–195 in East Providence, take Route 114 south into Barrington. The second river bridge that you drive over spans the Warren River, which serves as the town line separating Barrington and Warren.

Because the Warren and Barrington rivers are fork rivers that join, their estuarine nature, bait potential, and fishing opportunities are remarkably similar. Like the Barrington, the Warren has good bridge fishing from the same bike path that used to be a railroad bridge. The Route 114 bridge for both rivers is utilized on the outgoing tide; there is also good schoolie fishing farther upstream.

The Warren enjoys a slightly greater amount of tidal exchange but less access opportunity than the Barrington. With regard to

In late May and early June, look for monster stripers in the estuarine rivers like the Warren.

fishing from the bridges, the bike-path bridge has a slight edge and must be fished during the incoming tide. This is a short bridge, and it is a simple matter to walk a good catch to shore on either end for landing. Baits used are live or dead alewives (preferably fresh). Later, when the alewives are finished or hard to get, you can drift sea worms in the current, adding the correct amount of split shot to drift at the right level for stripers.

Naturally, if the incoming water holds fish, you can usually expect the outgoing to yield. However, the Route 114 bridge—for falling-tide fishing—presents tougher landing opportunities, and you'll have to do some fancy climbing down to the water if the bass you've got is a big one.

Few anglers know that the marshy shore north of the Warren River bike-path bridge can be highly productive casting from the east bank. During a falling tide, it is possible to throw a dead alewife upcurrent, permitting a drift until it is fully downtide, where big fish will pick it up and move off. A caster with a popping plug at dawn will bring up small fish on either tide, and I can think of no better spot for fly casting than the shallows on the east bank of the river above the trestle. Fly fishing works either tide, but a falling tide can mean big trouble if the lineside is a good one and you hook up too close to the bridge. If it were not for the smell of salt, you might imagine yourself on a river in Europe. At the right times, the river could be rated four, but this hot spot had to be penalized due to its short season. The best fish here, though not all that common, weigh in around the low forties, and one's chances for that kind of fish improve downriver.

Of less importance is a sizable white perch run in March; the perch can be taken way upriver in Seekonk, on the small backroad bridge just below I–195. Fish the bottom with a sea-worm bit.

TIP: The most common error that many otherwise competent fly fishers make is that they fail to understand the natural history of striped bass.

53
Bristol Narrows
Bristol, Rhode Island

BEST MONTHS TO FISH: May through July.

RECOMMENDED METHODS: Sea worms, alewives, swimming plugs, and fly fishing.

FISH YOU CAN EXPECT TO CATCH: Blackfish, stripers, and bluefish.

HOW TO GET THERE: Bristol Narrows is south of Warren. Take a left turn onto Narrows Road off Route 136 southbound.

Access to the Narrows, which is really the west bank of the mouth of the Kickemuit River, is by way of a sandbar that is exposed at low tide. People like to drive onto the bar either to launch their boats or to fish from shore. It is not soft or dangerous, but failure to move that vehicle when the tide begins coming back could spoil your day.

In late April, there is a blackfish spawning run that is Rhode Island's worst-kept secret. Shoulder to shoulder with fifty other fishermen, it is possible to fill a bucket with tautog ranging from 3 to 12 pounds. An absolute requirement is that you fish the outgoing tide with sea worms and never cast more than 30 feet. This is group sport where mutual cooperation is mandatory. Fish with a thick skin and be polite or the others will use you for bait—and they prefer chunks.

Other than an occasional couple of romantic kids, there is little activity at night here, but often the linesides of Mount Hope Bay will forage in the shallows or lurk in the currents that form from the Kickemuit River. Except for the aforementioned tautog fishing, which is all done during the day, any tide in which water is moving in the deep night when things are quiet has potential. A steady producer in spring through June is a dead alewife on a 7/0

If it's blackfish you're after, you can't go wrong on a dropping tide in early May in the Bristol Narrows.

hook (mono leader) drifted in the currents. Let any fish that picks it up move off 10 yards before whacking it. You can also do well with swimming plugs. In either case, because this river has an alewife run of its own that lures big bass up from Mount Hope Bay, be ready for some Moby linesides at times or you will cry. Because of the alewife run, spring has an edge, but I have still seen good stripers here all summer in lesser numbers. As is so much the case elsewhere, blues often take up slack left by stripers.

This is another great fly-rod spot because of its good wading, natural protection (to allay surf), and attractive currents. No hassles. Remember that if this were a tautog book, Bristol Narrows would be rated five.

CONTACT TIP: Sam's Bait and Tackle, (401) 848–5909, knows about the whole east bay.

54

Brenton Point State Park
Newport, Rhode Island

BEST MONTHS TO FISH: From July on, but especially October and November.

RECOMMENDED METHODS: Plugs, green crabs, or seaworms.

FISH YOU CAN EXPECT TO CATCH: Stripers, bluefish, and blackfish.

HOW TO GET THERE: Take Route 138 into Newport to the Farewell Street exit south, go left onto Memorial Boulevard, then take the second right onto Bellevue Avenue south (signs to mansions point this way as well), which ends at the beginning of Ocean Drive. First indication of easy access is

King's Beach Fishing Area, which is adjacent to Brenton Point.

This area offers a ½ mile of rocky shore that is excellent habitat for stripers and bluefish. While the coastal structure is similar to Narragansett's, the water here is more shallow, and perhaps less dangerous—but still good cover for stripers and baitfish in the nook-and-cranny shoreline. Regulars prefer eels, both live and rigged, along with swimming plugs. Day anglers—and their prospects get better as the season progresses—use poppers. Surfcasters who know how to read water can excel here. A hot item at this writing is the Mambo Minnow in the largest size. No particular tide favors this spot, but any moderate onshore wind—southeast to west—helps. Look for good blackfish opportunities with green crabs as bait in late October.

CONTACT TIP: Saltwater Edge, (401) 842–0062, is a great fly shop here that knows the ropes and takes fly fishers on guided trips.

55

Fort Adams State Park
Newport, Rhode Island

BEST MONTHS TO FISH: From July on, but especially October and November.

RECOMMENDED METHODS: Plugs.

FISH YOU CAN EXPECT TO CATCH: Stripers and bluefish.

HOW TO GET THERE: Continue along Ocean Drive from Brenton Point until you see signs for Fort Adams. Brenton Road out of Newport will also get you there.

Fort Adams is more protected, more into the bay, than Brenton Point. As a result, the flatter and shallower water that results from this often demands the cover of darkness for feeding stripers to use it. But, under the cover of darkness, there are feeding stripers and blues along the west edge of the park, which is the shore of Narragansett Bay's east passage. Entrance is sometimes limited at night, but officials generally do not deny access to people equipped for fishing at any hour. This spot is a good alternative if a nasty east wind should kick up, spoiling the fishing at Brenton Point. Also, menhaden, which frequent Narragansett Bay, will sometimes give this spot an edge. It is a good idea to combo up the Fort with Brenton and watch them both, as they are just far enough apart to provide similar though unique opportunities.

CONTACT TIP: Anglers using traditional methods can contact Beachfront Bait and Tackle, (401) 849–4665.

BLOCK ISLAND

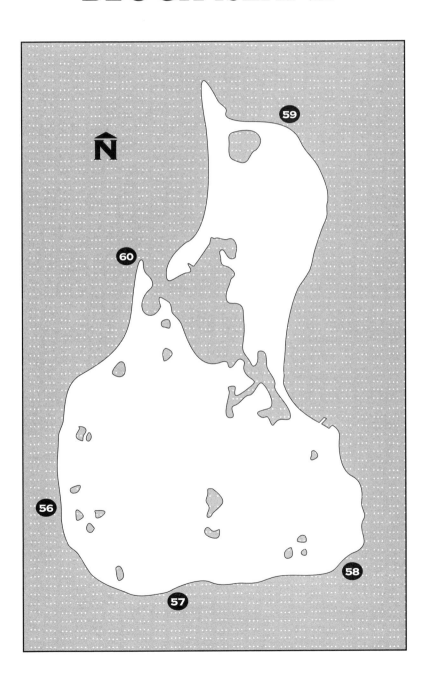

Just 17 miles east of Montauk and 12 miles south of Rhode Island, Block Island has only recently come into its own as an attractive, or at least well-known, surfcasting spot. During the late seventies and early eighties, when striper opportunities were drying up everywhere else, the "Block" provided some memorable encounters with Moby stripers. Indeed, it was probably the twilight of striper fishing's glory days.

I've had to make some painful decisions regarding exactly which spots to include here. In spite of overt efforts by some to protect a number of locations where shore fishing takes place regularly, I just had too many places. Safety was the reason for dropping Sandy Point; in the case of Mohegan Bluffs, I combined several related spots. Indeed, that whole south shore is so replete with points and coves as to render the area, much to my delight, one great hot spot.

The island is not a be-all and end-all location, because logistics raise the price of going there well beyond what some are willing to pay. There is only one ferry that carries autos in fall, and if the weather turns bad, that vessel may not run. Dyed-in-the-wool island fishermen like to keep one junker for their "inner circle" to use in the fall. (I wonder what Rhode Island's new mandatory insurance law will do to that tradition.) Others leave the family auto behind and one member loses transportation for a few weeks while the other takes daily flights out of Westerly. No doubt a string of consecutive storms, ending the season by sheer default of time, will send an angler on a retrieval trip that lacks the luster of having some fishing thrown in, what with Christmas so close. Renting a place for the season, the gang all tosses money into the pot; this is the least of all expenses.

There are fewer fish but more charm in summer, when the weather is safer. Ferries operate out of Newport and New London on a seasonal basis. The only year-round ferry, the one that keeps this place alive, comes daily from Galilee, Rhode Island, and it carries cars.

56

Southwest Point
Block Island, Rhode Island

BEST MONTHS TO FISH: June through November.

RECOMMENDED METHODS: Plugs.

FISH YOU CAN EXPECT TO CATCH: Stripers.

HOW TO GET THERE: From Old Harbor, take Ocean Avenue, then left onto Beach Avenue to a left onto Center Road. Take a right onto Cooneymus Road and follow it to land's end. There are any number of undeveloped trails that will lead to Southwest Point. All are complicated and some are even embroiled in legal controversy, but any left at the end of Cooneymus will lead to suitable parking. Walk the shore south, or left, until opposite a red bell buoy about 400 feet from shore. This marks Southwest Point.

Southwest Point is thought to be a very good spot on the island because it can provide opportunities for bigger stripers; however, this rocky shore can accommodate so few anglers that I am forced to rate it somewhat lower than I might otherwise. Past performance has given it a reputation for big bass that it can't always live up to. A maddening aspect of this spot, as with any productive spot of similar size, is that crowds have a way of ruining the fishing. Dropping tides are popular with southwest winds. Increase the rating by one or two for November fishing.

CONTACT TIP: Call Twin Maples, (401) 466–5547, for an island overview.

57

Mohegan Bluffs
Block Island, Rhode Island

BEST MONTHS TO FISH: June through November.

RECOMMENDED METHODS: Plugs.

FISH YOU CAN EXPECT TO CATCH: Stripers and bluefish.

HOW TO GET THERE: From Old Harbor, take Ocean Avenue, then left onto Beach Avenue to a left onto Center Road. After the airport, the road becomes Lakeside Drive, which you follow south for another mile to its end for a right onto Black Rock Road. You'll know the right turn because of the 3-foot painted stone at the intersection. Park where you can, at places where there is the greatest evidence of use. The road is close to the bluff at Black Rock.

This spot is really an area comprising three well-known hot spots: Black Rock, Spar Point, and Snake Hole. All provide a similar alternating rock-and-sand structure at the base of the south shore Mohegan Bluffs. Because there is so much here, the seasoned surfcaster can read for suitable striper-holding water and fish only what he or she likes. Like the roads leading here, none of these places has signs announcing its identity; once you've climbed down the cliffs, it is hard to locate suitable landmarks if you're not familiar with the rocky shoreline. While the fishing here is not quite as good as at Southwest Point, the area compensates with its ability to accommodate any number of anglers, which means plenty of room to fish in peace. Look for the blues to arrive in mid-July and improve with the season.

TIP: When changing flies or lures, shield your light from the foreground or you will spook linesides hell west and crooked.

Mohegan Bluffs is a good spot to find a combination of stripers and blues.

58

Southeast Light
Block Island, Rhode Island

BEST MONTHS TO FISH: August through November.
RECOMMENDED METHODS: Popping plugs.
FISH YOU CAN EXPECT TO CATCH: Bluefish and occasional stripers.
HOW TO GET THERE: From Old Harbor, go south on Southeast
Road until you reach public parking near the lighthouse.

This is a tough spot to climb down into, but when blues couldn't
be found anywhere else in the late sixties, I was catching them here
in daylight with poppers. The rocky shore is loaded with highly
readable water that also holds stripers, but don't expect them until
after dark. I suggest you become familiar with the shore by daylight
in one of those rare spots where you can have day fishing; then try
the stripers once you've learned your way around. They say that a
60-plus lineside was taken here in the early-eighties heyday of island fall fishing. But there is so much protectionism and fairy lore
here that few local anglers are willing to talk about anything, so I
doubt we'll ever know. My first Block Island striper—an 18-
pounder in 1969—came from between Mohegan Bluffs and the
lighthouse, an area sometimes called Corn Cove.

TIP: Never worry about stripers seeing in the dark. They have a
proximity sense, which is a combination of those senses we
understand and those we are still trying to figure out.

59

Grove Point
Block Island, Rhode Island

BEST MONTHS TO FISH: June through November.

RECOMMENDED METHODS: Plugs.

FISH YOU CAN EXPECT TO CATCH: Stripers and occasional bluefish.

HOW TO GET THERE: From Old Harbor, take Corn Neck Road north for nearly 4 miles. Once Sachem Pond is visible on your left, you'll see state land on the ocean side to your right just before the paved portion of the road ends.

You'll have to use a cast-and-walk system of feeling the place out, but the entire rocky shoreline in this area can hold stripers at times. I'm convinced that much of what was learned by surfcasters here was taught to them by boat fishermen who were just a little farther off shore. My old striper buddy, Ray Jobin, as competent a striper-man as I've ever known, did a job there regularly in the late sixties. If you can locate a mussel bar, the early incoming tide can be productive. Avoid an east wind unless it is light and in an early stage of development.

TIP: Never stand in one spot when working nondescript shore-lines. Rather, work the water by moving a few feet and direct casts toward structure.

60

Inlet to Great Salt Pond (the Cut)
Block Island, Rhode Island

BEST MONTHS TO FISH: June through November.

RECOMMENDED METHODS: Fly fishing, light spinning, and bait.

FISH YOU CAN EXPECT TO CATCH: Stripers, blues, bonito, little tuney, and fluke.

HOW TO GET THERE: Go west on Ocean Avenue, take a left onto Side Road for ½ mile, then go right on Champlins Road all the way out to the Coast Guard station. Park at the last corner.

The Coast Guard Channel of the salt pond into New Harbor, a close walking distance, is considered the best shore fishing spot on the island. The Cut, as it is fondly known, is most popular with fly anglers and pluggers who fish from the jetty to the Coast Guard Station. Best tides are reputed to be moving water, mid-tide, going either way. Though the target species remains stripers, fishing for bonito, and some years little tuney—two highly selective species— can be quite reliable. Small lures and flies seem to work best. Epoxy patterns are very popular in Great Salt Pond once the bonito appear. The jetty there is not suitable for fishing because of height from the water, condition of rocks, and the slime. Even if you hooked a good fish, you would never get it in.

Located south of the entrance to New Harbor's salt pond, the ½-mile sandy stretch of shore known as Charlestown Beach provides some good chunk fishing for bass at night and fluke fishing with chubs and squid strips during the day.

CONTACT TIP: Bruce Johnson runs an Orvis Shop, Oceans & Ponds, (401) 466–5131, which caters to fly fishing.

MARTHA'S VINEYARD

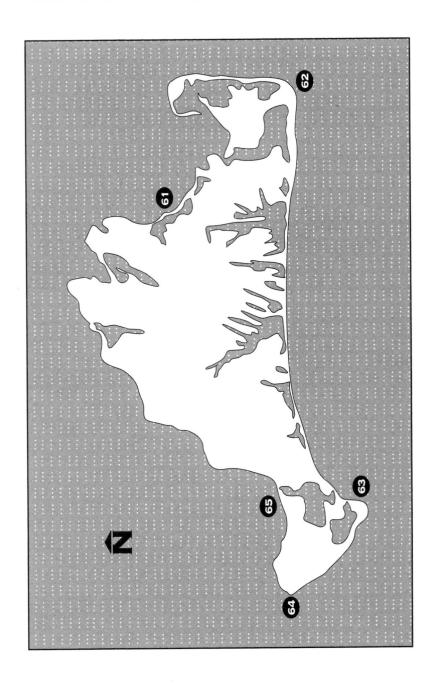

The late Bob Post, author of Reading the Water, *provided valuable information on the Vineyard.*

Of the offshore islands of consequence, each can lay claim to a certain unique quality: Block Island is largely undiscovered; Nantucket is the most charming; the Vineyard celebrates surfcasting with terrific enthusiasm. Very soon after one leaves the ferry, it becomes excitingly evident to any shore fisherman that surfcasting is alive and well on Martha's Vineyard. Pat Abate, an old-guard Cape surfcasting comrade from another life, says, "It's the only place I have ever gone where they cheer and embrace fishermen as though they were a high school team."

Part of the Vineyard that didn't make the cut was the entire south shore because so much of it is private property. I would like to have included a treatment of the great pond openings in spring, when the past year's alewives are panting to get out and the present season's are straining to make it in—stripers cutting through the emerald walls of sea while sweet water mingles. Another hard choice was Cape Poge, which had to be left out because of limited parking and difficult access, especially during the piping plover mating season.

I am, of course, indebted to the late Robert Post, the author of an unforgettably charming collection of Vineyard surf-fishing portraits in his book, *Reading the Water* (Globe Pequot). When reading Post, one develops an appreciation for both natural history and the island's rich lore. Indeed, he engages his reader on any number of levels while never losing touch with a simple, folksy style that irrevocably touches something in each of us. Yet the mission of worshipping at the altar of surfcasting is never more than a cast away. Thus, while you wend your way along the streets and shores of the Vineyard, you are unwittingly taking the medicine of enlightenment while tasting the sweetness of play. It is a Dr. Post skill that I feel privileged to share with you here.

61

Vineyard Bridges
Oak Bluffs and Edgartown,
Martha's Vineyard, Massachusetts

BEST MONTHS TO FISH: May, June, September, and October.

RECOMMENDED METHODS: Fly fishing, eels, jigs, small plugs, needlefish, Hopkins, and Kastmasters.

FISH YOU CAN EXPECT TO CATCH: Stripers, bluefish, bonito, and false albacore.

HOW TO GET THERE: Little Bridge, Joseph Sylvia State Beach, and Anthiers Bridge (also known as Big Bridge) are located on the northeast side of the island. Access and parking are available year-round parallel to the beach for 1½ miles. Take New York Avenue to Seaview Avenue, which becomes Beach Road. Little Bridge is located at the Oak Bluffs end of Beach Road, and Anthiers Bridge is at the Edgartown end. State Beach is between them.

Because this area faces Nantucket Sound, high surf is rare. Beach Road is really a paved-over barrier beach between the sound and Sengekontacket Pond, one of the primary sources of bay scallops on the Vineyard.

The inlets and jetties that serve the pond's water are located at each bridge, where baitfish are usually running in and out with the tides. What makes this stretch of beach unique is the variety of methods anglers can try here in their quest for hooking gamefish.

Bridge fishing is popular on Anthiers. One technique is to drift eels over the side by letting them run with the tide; this is especially effective with stripers and blues in the fall. Fish with an open bail, applying finger pressure to the line so that you can allow a short run before setting the hook. Then, carefully work yourself off the bridge so you can better fight and land a fish from the beach.

In the 1960s, the late author and inventor Al Reinfelder developed an effective technique for fishing his Bait Tail jigs from bridges. Favoring the uptide side of the bridge that faced the oncoming water, Al's technique required heavy tackle, what with the fish having the tendency to go with the current under the bridge and around the pilings. Al once wrote, "Fish take feeding positions on both sides of the bridge, but rarely in the middle, directly beneath the span. Since fish always face the current, those on the front of the bridge face away from the bridge, while those on the back face the bridge directly" (*Bait Tail Fishing,* 1969). This doesn't mean the angler won't get the attention of a striper on the "back side" of a bridge, but the chance of fighting and landing a fish successfully increases if one doesn't have to fight pilings and other bridge obstructions.

In early spring, some of the first schoolie stripers of the season arrive at Anthiers Bridge Inlet to Sengekontacket Pond. Fly-rod fishermen have success off the jetties and on the beach fronting the pond. Sand eel and 1-inch orange worm imitations (it is worm spawn-out time) work best. Spin fishermen should stick to light tackle with jigs or small swimmers. Late summer and fall fishing improves with the arrival of the daylight feeders—bonito and false albacore. These unpredictable gamesters can hit at any tide, but early morning outgoing or high slack seem to produce best. Flies, Swedish pimples, and needlefish should produce a hook-up.

The 1½-mile stretch of sandy beach between the bridges is also a fine area for bottom fishing with cut bait. Pick a pleasant fall night and bring a beach chair and a cooler with food and drink. After several minutes—or several hours—you may hook up with a monster bluefish or giant cow bass. Sometimes it pays to be innovative if the fish aren't hitting. Many years ago, a fisherman who had run through all his bait was left with nothing but a foil-wrapped cigar. After putting a hook through it, he dropped it over the side of Anthiers Bridge and caught a fine striped bass.

CONTACT TIP: Larry's Tackle Shop, (508) 627–5088, is a Vineyard fly-fishing headquarters.

62

Wasque Point

Edgartown, Martha's Vineyard, Massachusetts

BEST MONTHS TO FISH: May through November.

RECOMMENDED METHODS: Joppa Jigs, swimming plugs, eels, tins, and popping plugs.

FISH YOU CAN EXPECT TO CATCH: Stripers and bluefish.

HOW TO GET THERE: If using a buggy, take a right off Main Street in Edgartown onto Katama Road and follow it to land's end at South Beach. There, on the left, you'll find a marked beach path for vehicles. Those without a beach vehicle can take a left onto North Water Street, then a left onto Daggett for the Chappy Ferry. Once across, take Chappaquiddick Road for 2½ miles to a right onto Poucha Road and then a left onto Wasque Road (dirt road), where there is a Trustees of Reservation booth marking the entrance to Wasque. Anglers with their gear can walk the ⅗₀ mile to the sandy beach along a marked path.

Open water and Nantucket Sound collide at Wasque, forming a tremendous rip. The last four hours of a falling tide (east to west) are the most popular. Regulars particularly like this tide when it combines with a strong southwest wind, which causes the rip to kick up, making bait more vulnerable and seemingly causing game-fish to attack more reliably.

Because of the crowds that collect there when stripers and blues are running, artificials are the only method that can be used. (Some will fish bait briefly among light crowds at slack tide.) Occasional stripers are taken during the day, but Wasque's better fish usually hit at night. In spring, it is a case of watching for bait arrivals—herring, then squid. By then, there should be a good striper population surging through the rips. Joppa jigs, which are produced locally, work magic during the first arrivals. Then Gibbs Swimmers, Atoms, and Dannys dominate, as the linesides get bigger with the progressing season.

Bluefish, it seems, hold up all summer, providing fairly consistent action even during the day. Hopkins, Kastmasters, Ballistic Missiles, Roberts Casting Plugs, and Atom poppers—all chosen to

From mid-summer on, you can catch fish any time of day at Wasque Point.

produce casting distance—will bring them up. Hooked fish take advantage of the current running strong to the right. Let downtide surfcasters know that you are on and that you are coming down so that you can safely follow and keep the fish in front of you. They should be willing to reel in line and yield.

While the fishing is predominantly blues and stripers (in that order), bonito and false albacore are sometimes taken during August and September, but these are uncommon showings. Similarly, on October 30, 1986, Dan Colli hooked and landed a 68-pound yellowfin tuna on a Spofford Ballistic Missile while casting for bluefish. In the late 1960s, islander Dick Hathaway almost landed a giant sturgeon, estimated to weigh around 200 pounds.

To use a buggy, both a Dukes County beach sticker and a Wasque Point Trustees of Reservation Oversand Vehicle Permit are required. Obey all regulations because rare or endangered piping plovers or least terns may be nesting. As a result, this spot is definitely subject to intermittent closings as various branches of government and private interests grapple with management of endangered bird species. It may be necessary to check on the status of Wasque through tackle shops or the Chamber of Commerce.

CONTACT TIP: Dick's Bait and Tackle, (508) 693–7669, in Oak Bluffs can report on Vineyard surf fishing.

63
Squibnocket Point
Chilmark, Martha's Vineyard, Massachusetts

BEST MONTHS TO FISH: May through mid-June, and mid-September through mid-November.

RECOMMENDED METHODS: Large swimming plugs and eels.

FISH YOU CAN EXPECT TO CATCH: Stripers and bluefish.

HOW TO GET THERE: Head southwest on State Road to South Road in Chilmark. Two miles past Beetlebung Corner, take a left onto Squibnocket Road (marked by a granite pillar). This road ends at the town parking lot on Squibnocket Bight. The lot is restricted to town residents during the summer tourist season.

To the right of the parking lot is a 2-mile stretch of excellent striper fishing. Start by casting in "The Bowl"—to the right of the parking area—on the incoming tide at dusk, then work your way down to the "Mussel Bed." This is the same area described by Jerry Jansen, surf-fishing pioneer and author of *Successful Surf Fishing,* published in 1934:

> Bait fish are almost always present in "The Bowl," and in the fall this spot is absolutely thick with bait. . . . Extending around the bowl is a rock and sand bar covered with mussel beds. This bar is a highly favored spot, and it can be waded from dead low tide until the rising water gets too rough. Don't try this unless you are in the company of someone who has been out there a few times. . . . The best tide here is the rising and as much of it as you can stand. No matter what the tide, however, get there before sunup and stick it out until daylight. If the fish are going to hit, they will do so before light and will quit right after it gets light enough to see. The Mussel Bed is a prime spot for night fishing. All the beach up to Squibnocket Point is excellent, being full of the rocks and holes so dearly loved by bass and surf anglers. Around the point, the "beach" is a sloping wall of round rocks with a few sandy spots here and there. It is an excellent place to fish, but you may run into private property.

Remember that the Massachusetts Colonial Ordinance (1641–47) gave anglers the right of trespass. "The public may also pass over privately owned land below the mean high-tide mark for the purpose of fishing, fowling, and navigation. The courts have ruled, however, that walking the beach and bathing are not among the public rights in the intertidal zone" (source: "Public Access to the Waters of Massachusetts," Department of Fisheries, Wildlife, and Environmental Law Enforcement, page 2). Nevertheless, I avoid using this spot during the bathing season.

In the late 1800s, Squibnocket Point was the location of two prestigious bass clubs: the Squibnocket Club, with eight bass stands, and the Providence Club, with three. These provided a gathering place to fish and socialize in the period following the Civil War. "Stands for the most part were made by driving steel rods into the rocks to support narrow wooden walkways. At the end of each walkway was a small platform from which the angler cast" (from *The Complete Book of Striped Bass Fishing,* Hal Lyman and Frank Woolner). A chummer and a gaffer assisted the angler. The clubs died out around 1897, when striped bass went into one of their notorious periods of population decline and almost vanished from the New England coast.

Although plugging at night will usually produce only striped bass and an occasional bluefish, in 1983 Vineyard fisherman Whit Manter hooked up to a shark on a Danny plug. After a heart-pounding, knee-knocking battle, the 212-pound, 7-foot 9-inch monster was landed.

TIP: Fine that you know where to fish for stripers, but do you know how? Did you read *Striper Surf?*

64

Gay Head Cliffs/Pilots Landing
Gay Head, Martha's Vineyard, Massachusetts

BEST MONTHS TO FISH: June, July, October, and November.

RECOMMENDED METHODS: Poppers, swimming plugs, eels, and large black needlefish.

FISH YOU CAN EXPECT TO CATCH: Stripers and bluefish.

HOW TO GET THERE: Located on the southwest facing side of the Vineyard, this area is reached by taking State Road to South Road, which ends in a loop. At the bottom of the loop, across from public rest rooms, there is town parking that anglers can use evenings. To the right of the parking lot is the beach access boardwalk, which is owned by the Martha's Vineyard Land Bank, and which you have to stay on.

Once on the beach, walk ½ mile to the right to Southwest Rock. At this point, on a coming tide, the Atlantic sweeps into Vineyard Sound, creating a small rip off the point. If you keep walking right, you'll find the next ½ mile to be prime fishing. Fish the rock piles, the bowl, and the next point, which is Pilots Landing. Gay Head Cliffs and Pilots Landing are dusk-to-dawn hot spots. Change of light may produce on any tide, but top of the tide—last two hours of incoming—will produce best through the night. Checking the type of bait in the water could help you with lure selection. Nights when mullet have been visible, large swimming plugs have produced. If sand eels are abundant, try a needlefish, an eel, or a teaser fly tied off a barrel swivel in front of a swimming plug.

The cliffs here are a national treasure and landmark. Rising 150 feet from sea level, they are the highest cliffs on the Atlantic Coast, and a lighthouse stands guard at the peak. The varied colors of the clay that slopes down to the beach make for a spectacular fishing spot. Once part of the Algonquin nation, these cliffs are now within the Gay Head Wampanoag Indian Lands. The fragile cliffs are considered sacred ground by the Indians, so do not attempt to walk down them. Also, it is dangerous and contributes to erosion.

In the 1950s, it was not uncommon to catch codfish and pollock from the surf here. Vineyard fisherman Kib Bramhall recalls pollock being so abundant that a Pollock Derby ran the week after the Striped Bass and Bluefish Derby ended. Bramhall says, "It centered around Menemsha and Gay Head and was run by Manuel Lima, who was an ardent islander fisherman." From the late 1970s until 1984, weakfish made a return and were abundant, enabling anglers to catch stripers, blues, and weaks in a single trip.

TIP: The mullet run is the silent event of the northern part of its range. You only hear about it in New Jersey and the offshore islands, but it also occurs on the Cape and Rhode Island. September is best.

65

Lobsterville Beach and Jetty
Gay Head, Martha's Vineyard, Massachusetts

BEST MONTHS TO FISH: June through October.

RECOMMENDED METHODS: Joppa Jigs, small swimming plugs, Swedish Pimples, eels, fresh bait, and fly fishing.

FISH YOU CAN EXPECT TO CATCH: Stripers, bluefish, bonito, and false albacore.

HOW TO GET THERE: Lobsterville Beach is located on the northwest side (but to the southwest) fronting Vineyard South and Menemsha Bight. Take State Road to South Road, then right onto Lobsterville Road. Go ¾ mile to "Bend-in-the-Road," which is a public parking area for Town Beach. To reach the jetty at Menemsha Pond, continue along Lobsterville Road and bear left onto West Basin Road. There are marked parking spaces near the jetty. Be sure to observe the NO PARKING signs along these roads.

From the Town Beach parking area, anglers can walk ¾ mile to the left until they reach Dogfish Bar, or they can walk 1½ miles to the right to the jetties. The entire beach will produce, but the fishing will improve as concentrations of bait increase. Calm water and an abundance of baitfish moving in and out of Menemsha Pond have made this area one of the premier fly-fishing spots on the East Coast. White and yellow Lefty Deceivers work best.

Spring is best for school stripers. Later in the season, locals like a falling tide after dark. In August, big bass often go up into the pond across from the Coast Guard station. There are good results here at night casting eels, or, if you can snag some bunker (pogie), drift them live in the channel. Stay in free spool or open bail with a finger controlling the line, and when you feel it move off from a take, count to ten and give it a whack. I often use a double-hook setup for blues, which, when they go into a frenzy, will often share the pogie so that you can catch two at once. With blues, use wire leaders of 50- or 80-pound test. For stripers, 50-pound mono leaders are preferred.

While the blues hit best at dawn and dusk, bonito and false albacore feed during the day at the jetty from late July until mid-October. Because they are unpredictable and finicky feeders, plan on spending many hours seeking a hookup. But we've found that fresh bait—such as tinker mackerel and sand eels—on a number 8 or 10 treble hook works well. Of artificials, the most successful are the Spofford Needlefish with a slow retriever and the Swedish Pimple with a very rapid one.

Calm nights on the pond, when the water is clear, check for bait. Instead of sand eels, you may be rewarded with the rare sighting of a baby lobster migration on the ocean floor.

TIP: While floating fly lines will serve 90 percent of your fly-casting needs, have a fast or extra-fast sink line for the deep water spots on flats where bass are grubbing or tailing. It is also a spare that will fill in for disasters.

NANTUCKET

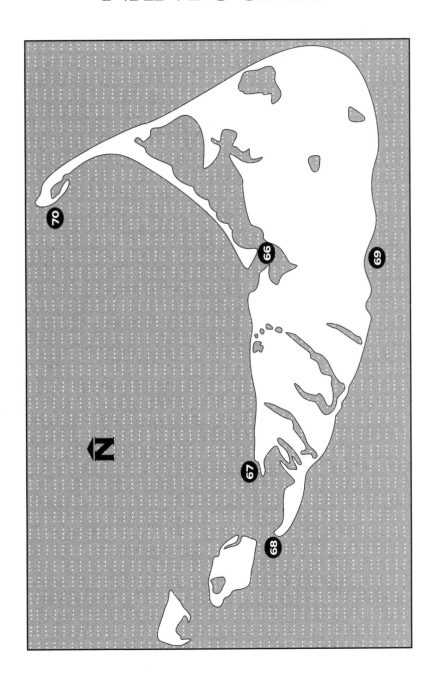

The tendency to group the offshore islands of Nantucket and Martha's Vineyard is without basis. All similarity ends after addressing the fact that they are both islands. Nantucket is more distinctive, slightly more exclusive, and certainly farther to sea. Comparisons between the two crop up incessantly. I would never dare publicly take a position as to which had the better surfcasting. The one arbitrary call I am tempted to make is that there are more bluefish, bonito, and albacore on Nantucket than anywhere else, and this is because of the isle's proximity to the Gulf Stream, which gives it access to more tropical species and lengthens its season.

While nervously plodding the gangway ashore, it's hard to avoid the sense of having come to some strange and distant place. Dedication to fishing oozes from every cultural cue: Well-manicured charter vessels crowd the docks to serve those willing to fish for just anything; and there are just enough buggies—fly rods on the roof racks—sprinkled amid the busy streets to prove that there are still some people who know exactly what they are fishing for and that surfcasting is alive and well on Nantucket.

Unique to Nantucket is the fact that four out of five hot spots required the use of a buggy. Yet Brant Point, where one is not needed, was rated four by me—even though everyone I spoke to about it gave it five. I simply could not put Brant Point up there with Montauk or Plum Island.

66

Brant Point
Nantucket, Massachusetts

BEST MONTHS TO FISH: June through October.

RECOMMENDED METHODS: Live bait and fly fishing.

FISH YOU CAN EXPECT TO CATCH: Stripers.

HOW TO GET THERE: From the ferry dock, take a right onto South Beach, then right onto Easton Street. Officials are sensitive about illegal parking, so park up near the rotary.

When arriving by ferry, Brant Point is just about the first thing you see. It is the picturesque lighthouse on the west side (right) of the harbor opening. Tradition and experience dictate that the only thing to use here is live bait: alewives (in late May and surely most of June); whole bunkers and mackerel, and if the live article is not available, drifted dead; or live eels. The big attraction of this spot is that while strong currents are common here, the ferry, when it turns, reverses one engine and powers the other in a routine that drills an 18- to 35-foot-deep hole—only casting distance from shore. Moreover, bait is forced closer to the protected beach by the periodic action of ferry arrivals.

Chances of a 40- or 50-pounder are better here than anywhere else on Nantucket, and nights are best because of reduced boat traffic.

Immediately west of the point there is excellent fly fishing on the flats and on the sand bar inside the west jetty. Timing is the lower drop, mid-tide down. You don't need a buggy to fish here.

This is a quality rather than quantity spot. You come here with a single mission in mind: Mr. Big.

CONTACT TIP: Bill Pew of Fisher's Tackle, (508) 228–2261, has the Nantucket story.

67

Eel Point/Knuckles (Dionis)
Nantucket, Massachusetts

BEST MONTHS TO FISH: June through October.

RECOMMENDED METHODS: Plugs and fly fishing.

FISH YOU CAN EXPECT TO CATCH: Stripers and bluefish.

HOW TO GET THERE: Turn west from Main Street onto Madaket Road, then take a right onto Eel Point Road; at land's end, turn left (west). (Oversand vehicle necessary.)

This largely protected sand beach area is on the north shore of the west end. Extensive shallows that wind around the bend of Eel Point and into Madaket Harbor provide a bait-holding feature and the opportunity for wading vast flats that often hold good numbers of stripers in the deep of night. This "flat water" fishing appeals particularly to the army of new saltwater fly fishers at Nantucket. Spared from an eastern exposure, it is a great spot for escaping the early part of any impending storm. Of course, there are blues here, but they are decidedly secondary to the stripers.

The top two hours of the tide are popular at Eel Point. Remember also that here a humping sou'west, though in your face, will bring activity close in to the beach. Locals call all of this area Dionis, but that can lead to confusion for us outsiders, because the real fishing is on the west, toward Eel Point, not at the Dionis Beach where they bathe in shallows that are not the basis for this spot's reputation among surfcasters.

CONTACT TIP: For a second opinion call Barry Thurston's Tackle Shop, (508) 228–9595.

68

Smith Point
Nantucket, Massachusetts

BEST MONTHS TO FISH: May through November.

RECOMMENDED METHODS: Plug fishing and some fly fishing.

FISH YOU CAN EXPECT TO CATCH: Stripers and bluefish.

HOW TO GET THERE: Turn west from Main Street onto Madaket Road, then take a right onto Ames Avenue; at a dirt crossing, turn right for the beach. (Oversand vehicle recommended.)

This sou'west-facing corner of the island usually enjoys gentle on-shore winds and a steady dole of currents; both sweep the island and Madaket Harbor. At Smith Point proper, there is always a strong tide rip leaving the shore. This is a popular spot that often collects anglers for reasons that are obvious to any striper zealot, but wait—there's more: The protected, more estuarine Madaket flats appeal to fly rodders and Rebel, Red-fin, and other light plugcasters. From the beach access road out to the point, a distance of about 2 miles, you will see any number of bars and holes that invite serious surf-casters to exercise their beach-reading skills. Some of these spots enjoy local names and draw good numbers of anglers. While plug-fishing the open beach is the most popular, there is some baitfishing both very early and very late in the season. June and October are the prime months for migrating stripers to visit the island. In between, stray stripers and a late July onslaught of bluefish keep things interesting. A rising tide has an edge here, but right at Smith Point there is a good rip on the falling tide as well. The area where buggies come onto the beach can be fished without a buggy.

TIP: Be whispy when dressing streamer flies to avoid overly bushy whisk-broom-like creations.

69

Surfside Beach (Miacomet Pond)
Nantucket, Massachusetts

BEST MONTHS TO FISH: June through October.

RECOMMENDED METHODS: Plugs.

FISH YOU CAN EXPECT TO CATCH: Stripers and bluefish.

HOW TO GET THERE: Take Surfside Road south from town to land's end. Travel west on the beach from there. (Oversand vehicle required.)

East of the Smith Point beach area, or, if you cut left when going for Smith, the nearly 4-mile stretch of south shore can be read and worked to the max. I say that because this is where people who know their striper Ps and Qs like to go a-huntin'. They apply their previous knowledge of the local shore, read the beach, and use a system of probing—a cast here and a cast there. Besides cliffs that prevent easy access by foot, the sand along here can be soft as well as washed out. Thus, any beach buggy operator should be experienced in oversand operation. Because the sands shift on a year-to-year basis, it is a location where you can lose a vehicle. It's no place to start out developing skills. Like Smith Point, prevailing winds keep this a reasonably safe spot. Incoming water is more popular, but, as I've learned elsewhere, any time one tide is good, the other is never half bad. Good chase-me, catch-me running the beach in fall up to early November.

TIP: When fishing heavier than 20-pound test line, it is necessary to convert your equipment to revolving spool and that demands an educated thumb.,

70

Great Point
Nantucket, Massachusetts

BEST MONTHS TO FISH: July through October.

RECOMMENDED METHODS: Surface poppers, which are often chosen for casting qualities.

FISH YOU CAN EXPECT TO CATCH: Bluefish, stripers, and occasional bonito.

HOW TO GET THERE: Go east out of town on either Orange or Pleasant streets, both of which become Milestone Road, on which you travel a short distance. Go left onto Polpis Road. Continue for 3½ miles until you arrive at a left turn for Wauwinet Road. Here you'll come upon a gate house operated by the reservation trustees where they sell beach-vehicle permits, maps, and regulations for Great Point. (Oversand vehicle required.)

Reaching out from the northeast corner of the island, Great Point is a collision center for a dozen currents that don't have a clue

The rips and bluefish of Great Point never quit.

where they are going. This mass confusion of water is often clapping into the sky (depending on the wind) and producing a tide rip one is not likely to forget. It has to be one of the most visually stimulating surfcasting spots in this book. In season, it seems that there are always bluefish to be caught, regardless of tide or time of day. Daylight hours often enjoy a greater popularity, as surfcasters find it such a welcome novelty to fish in a world where they can see.

With blues the number-one quarry, the game here is casting a surface popper as far as you can, not only to cover more water, but also to splash through a patch of surface that the fellow beside you can't reach. Consequently, Polaris, Roberts Casting Plugs, and the native (and famous) Nantucket Rabbit—all designed to throw a mile now and catch later—dominate techniques. Light lines on large spools, which deplete less on the cast, are used by some to extend their range. On occasion, some opportunists, bored with conventional methods, might reach for a fly rod when action is close.

Of course, if it's on Nantucket, it's got to be a striper spot at some point, and Great Point does have its striper nights—probably June and October. But striper fishing from shore is not what gives the point its place of honor. (It lost one in its rating because of that.) Similarly, anyone coming here in the hope of beaching a bonito is apt to be disappointed. Nevertheless, although such an event is rare at any shore location, it is statistically more likely to happen here than elsewhere.

TIP: Never strike a heard or seen hit; wait until you feel the take.

CAPE COD CANAL

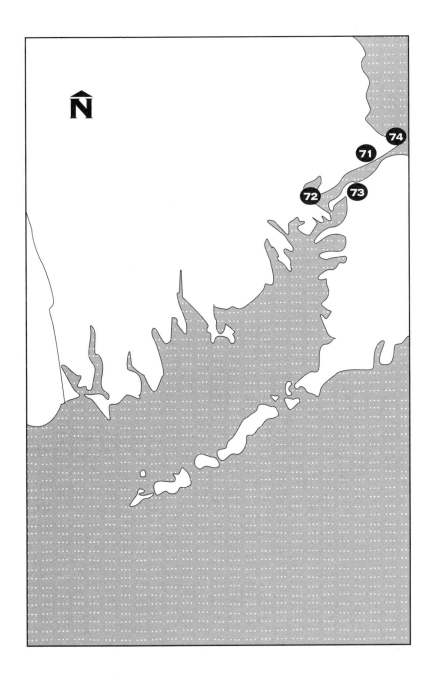

At just under 8 miles long, and averaging 600 feet wide, the Cape Cod Canal, which was planned to accommodate vessels drafting less than 30 feet, offers more productive striper spots for its area than any other location on the Striper Coast. Indeed, the four hot spots listed here are intended only to represent dozens more unlisted Canal locations, because I dare not consume too many pages of this work with the Canal alone. The result, were I to do so, would be boring duplication. How many times can I say the same things when listing the "Portigy Hole," Aptuxit, Jungle, Cribin, or Murderer's Row, to name only some? The methods and conditions for them are so similar that they would only further mire all efforts to avoid repetitiveness. I prefer to treat those that are unique in the numbered sections and utilize this general introduction for a broad discussion of the Canal's shore fishing. For instance, in every Canal spot where surfcasters gather, chunks of bunker or mackerel, fresh or frozen, are fished on the bottom. This method is currently state-of-the-art Canal fishing and begs a certain amount of social interpretation.

In my life on the Striper Coast, I have witnessed profound transitions in angling methods everywhere, but nowhere have they been as drastic as here. Thirty years ago, the Canal was frequented by a highly sophisticated, esoteric group of hard-cores who believed in fishing with the rod in hand and casting artificials. Then, they "skinned" the Canal by throwing eel-skin rigs that were hollow, cast well, and sank to strike-inducing depths. Making behavioral observations about striper movements and problem solving were accepted aspects of the sport. Today, a high percentage—though certainly not all—of Canal anglers are content to wait beside a chunk-baited rod. Those who do this, and I have no problem with it, will argue that chunking is what works best. I submit, however, that this is a case of self-fulfilling prophecy. If there is a failing to this kind of baitfishing, it is that it fails to cover water and it lacks mobility.

Many of the old-time Canal surfcasters used a bicycle, complete with bumper spikes similar to those on a buggy, to travel the tow roads along the banks. Such sense and innovation was their way of dealing with rules forbidding motor vehicles. That kind of enthusiasm is rare today. To spot cast to breaking fish chasing whiting, serious anglers carried a stack of rods. If a plug fell off the mark of a breaking fish, the caster needed only to drop the first stick and let fly with another. Such target work with repeating weapons saves time. Most important, these methods were the product of well-thought-out fishing strategies. But the door swings both ways: the rocket scientists of the time were not smart enough to fly fish.

But if this contrast between generations teaches us anything, it is that a whole new legion of virgin surfcasters is coming along, most of them born of the recovery of striped bass as a viable gamefish in the late eighties. Some of them will bring something new, and others will stick doggedly to tradition, while the wiser ones will draw from the best of both worlds.

The Cape Cod Canal of thirty years ago was a well-known hot spot of the Striper Coast. In the interim, however, the place fell out of favor, killing a couple of old-time tackle shops in the process and proving that just about everything on this planet is destined to repeat a cycle of ups and downs. One need only tip a curious head in observation in order to recognize the rediscovery of the Canal, even chuckle over the whispered praises uttered excitedly any place where surfcasters gather, to appreciate that we have gone full circle there in our devotions at the altar of striper fishing.

71

Herring Run
Cape Cod Canal, Bourne, Massachusetts

BEST MONTHS TO FISH: Late May and early June.

RECOMMENDED METHODS: Live alewives.

FISH YOU CAN EXPECT TO CATCH: Stripers.

HOW TO GET THERE: Take Route 25 to exit 2 (Bourne); then, from the rotary, follow Route 6 east along the north bank of the Canal for 2¼ miles.

The Canal Herring Run is a small stream that empties into the Canal at a state park on Route 6. Alewives, which are an anadromous fish engaged in a spawning run that begins in early April, run upstream until early June, and spent fish—those coming back downstream to the sea—drop back until mid-June. Also known locally as "herring," these 8- to 10-inch silvery baitfish provide foraging opportunities for stripers. Anglers take advantage of this situation by dip-netting herring, placing a hook on their nose, and swimming them live from the rocky banks of the Canal to waiting stripers. This is a high-profile spot on public land where parking, picnic tables, and rest rooms are provided. Even when the fishing is poor, there are anglers here around the clock.

The technique for using live alewives is somewhat specialized and requires special equipment. You'll need a landing net with a handle of 5 feet or longer, a hoop diameter of around 2 feet, and a small enough mesh size to keep the small baitfish. Once the herring have been caught, they have to be kept alive in a live bait box that is drifted in the Canal. Any container that allows an exchange of water and floats will do. Most regulars use a plastic laundry basket with a fitted plywood top that has a door with corrosion resistant hinges. Styrofoam flotation is installed under the top to keep the basket riding while the baitfish swim in new water. Anglers line the Canal banks, throwing live baits that have been hooked in the nose or back with a single 7/0 hook, then allowed to swim in the currents. It is best to allow any take, which is a sudden and feisty moving off of the bait, to swim 30 feet or so before striking back; hopefully the lineside will have the bait in his mouth by then.

The first keepable stripers are usually caught around May 20, and the really large brutes, say around 40 pounds, June 1. The later in the season, the better are the opportunities for big fish, until the herring are gone in mid-June. On any given day, the best action occurs during slack tide for about an hour; there are four of these per day. To compute Herring Run slack tide, subtract two hours from Boston, high or low tide; or add one hour and forty-five

Striper fishing, day and night, is a harbinger of spring at the Herring Run.

minutes to Providence, high or low tide. You can take stripers during the day here, but, as is so often the case, the night will be far more productive.

The limit for taking herring is twelve per day; taking herring is not permitted between 8:00 A.M. and 5:00 P.M., and a permit, issued at Town Hall in Bourne for $10, is required.

CONTACT TIP: Call the old and reliable Red Top Sporting Goods, (508) 759–3371, for information.

72

Massachusetts Maritime Academy
Cape Cod Canal, Bourne, Massachusetts

BEST MONTHS TO FISH: June through October.

RECOMMENDED METHODS: Swimming plugs and fly fishing.

FISH YOU CAN EXPECT TO CATCH: Stripers and bluefish.

HOW TO GET THERE: From Main Street in Bourne, turn south, toward the Canal, at the traffic light onto Academy Drive.

Massachusetts Maritime Academy is located on the north bank at the west end. Here the Canal widens and eddies, causing the currents to subside where pockets of slower water act as a haven for bait. Thus, while gamefish can pass you at any point in the "ditch," they are more likely to stop in this area. Also, unlike most of the rest of the Canal, it is shallow enough to do some wading, with suitable room for the backcast of a fly fisher. Among more traditional methods, small plugs tied direct to simulate sperling work well in the deep of night. The last two hours of the dropping tide are my favorites here.

The section of Canal bank belonging to the Academy is closed to parking from 10:00 P.M. to 6:00 A.M.; it is possible, however, to tuck one's vehicle elsewhere and walk the tow road for areas east of there that share the same shoreline characteristics.

CONTACT TIP: Maco's Bait and Tackle, (508) 759–9836, can help you.

73
Mud Flats (Tidal Flats Recreational Area)
Cape Cod Canal, Bourne, Massachusetts

BEST MONTHS TO FISH: June through October.

RECOMMENDED METHODS: Plugs, chunks, live eels, jigs, and fly fishing.

FISH YOU CAN EXPECT TO CATCH: Stripers and bluefish.

HOW TO GET THERE: After crossing the Bourne Bridge (Route 28), take a right onto Trowbridge Road from the rotary. At the next intersection, take a right onto Shore Road. Watch on your right for Bell Road, which leads to a pair of Corps of Engineers parking areas.

The Mud Flats, as they are fondly known by Canal regulars, are a departure from usual Canal banks, as there is a cove at the west end of this area. During high tide, bait gathers and gamefish will come in to take it. Once the tide starts dropping, it is possible to follow an imaginary line—it would be a continuation of the Canal bank—out on the flats for better plugcasting or fly-fishing opportunities in both directions. Of course, surfcasters are taking a chance here when they venture out too soon in deep-of-night striper fishing. Too far left into the cove is already dangerous, but too far right toward the Canal can be deadly. Listen to your fears; allow the tide to drop a little more each time when you begin here, and go out behind someone who has done it before. Once comfortable with flats-wading in the night, you will recognize that an early arrival to the west, or far end, of the flats can produce opportunities for the hungriest and greatest number of stripers. At the shore end, dry with the usual Canal rocky shore, many like to fish a menhaden or mackerel chunk on the bottom; some will bounce worms on the bottom.

TIP: To free drift a chunk in Canal currents, use an egg sinker above your leader barrel to get down.

74

East End

Cape Cod Canal, Sandwich, Massachusetts

BEST MONTHS TO FISH: July through September.

RECOMMENDED METHODS: Big plugs, chunks, and fly fishing.

FISH YOU CAN EXPECT TO CATCH: Stripers.

HOW TO GET THERE: From the north rotary of the Sagamore Bridge, where routes 6 and 3 intersect, follow signs east to Scusset Beach. Park as deep and as far right as you can to be near the Canal.

Just about all the stripers that summer in Cape Cod Bay will show up, sooner or later, lounging in the currents of the east end of the Canal. Long-time regulars will tell you that the rule is to be at this end during east, or falling, tides; however, the system works best when the tide is falling through the dawn. What that means is that a Boston high tide of 11:00 P.M. to midnight, which will have water flowing east during the dawn, is an excellent starting point for anyone hoping to intercept a Moby striper on a feeding safari. Once the water begins to slow down, however, the fishing is over.

Look for nice linesides like this one on the morning tides at the east end.

During those seasons, when there are good populations of whiting or squid, it is possible to witness the awesome force of a big bass beating the surface of the Canal in pursuit of breakfast. The first time I saw it, I thought a mule had been dropped from the Sagamore Bridge.

Use highly castable, overweight swimmers—such as loaded Atoms, Dannys, or Pikies—during the darkened hours and keep an ear cocked for the sound of thrashing fish. Once first light is in evidence, shift to poppers that will reach as far into the ditch as possible. Reverse Atoms, Gibb's Polaris, and oversized Striper Swipers should be used not only for their castability but also for their size. The trick here is to spot-cast a feeding fish as quickly as possible. Speed and accuracy count! Old stand-bys such as floater Rebels, with or without teasers, or 9-inch Slig-Gos will take those that are already in range.

Climb down the rocks beneath the last amber Canal light, then walk the sandy shore east beneath the breakwater; at this stage of the tide—low at dawn—the water is shallow enough to both pass and wade comfortably. Regulars will set up to fish the bottom with chunks just east of the rocky shoal under the light. Pluggers and fly fishers can wade east of there and still be in excellent water.

TIP: Most surfcasters don't know how much room fly casters need behind them. Pass cautiously.

MASSACHUSETTS

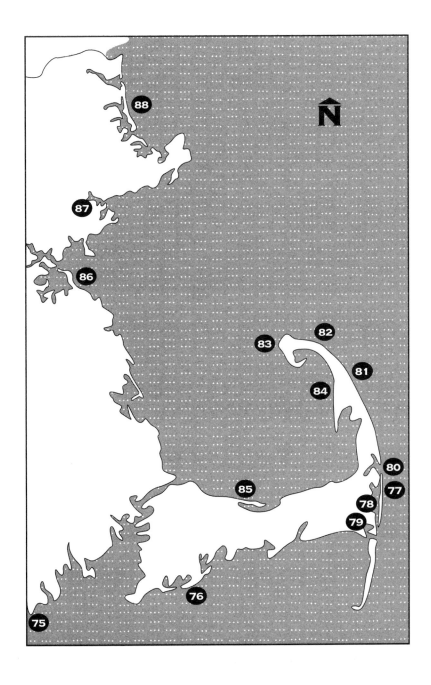

As the geographic center of the Striper Coast, Massachusetts leads the list of striper states by any measurement you choose. It offers the highest level of striper fishing, because it is most suitably situated to intercept the migration routes of both races of linesides—those of the Hudson and of the Chesapeake. It combines an enhanced level of access with a suitable coastline for holding linesides. Moreover, opportunities for other species certainly match, if not exceed, those found elsewhere. In addition to yielding Charles Church's All-Tackle World Record, which held for over fifty years, the Bay State boasts more 70-pound-plus striper landings than any other. Besides mainland Massachusetts, the Canal, Cape, and islands combine to offer the shore fisherman twenty-eight hot spots. Needless to say, if I could have only one striper state, this would be it.

Those of us who study the influence of environment on fishing know that there are two sets of climatic conditions in Massachusetts, where water temperatures can be dramatically different. By midsummer, the Gulf of Maine and Nantucket Sound are reading a difference of ten degrees or more, a factor that plays no small part in the determination of arrivals and departures of all marine species. For the shore fisherman, the line of temperature gradient occurs on either side of Monomoy Island, on the southeast corner of Cape Cod. Because of these differences, it is possible to frolic in the tepid waters of Nantucket Sound at seventy degrees in August while your counterpart is chipping his teeth in the suds of Nauset Beach—5 miles east as the gull flies—where the water is in the mid-fifties. Thus, north-shore striper arrivals and departures are trimmed by two or more weeks at each end of the season.

But the Bay State is not all buttercups and breezes: witness, for example, the death of Cape Cod surf fishing. Under the guise of "management," the Cape Cod National Seashore caretakes the entire Outer Cape under a closure (imposed in 1985) that prohibits use of an oversand vehicle on the beaches there for all but 7 of 47 miles. Under this management plan, it is impossible to carry equipment the vast distances involved, let alone carry a fish out.

At this writing, Mike Perel, Provincetown selectman and a surf fisherman who is on the Seashore Park Advisory Board, is working to design a more reasonable beach utilization plan that would include vehicle access at night during summer and all day during the off-season, particularly in the fall. While some compromise plan is in the offing, I cannot say, long-term, whether the Outer Cape will ever reclaim its place as the finest surfcasting location on the planet.

With one exception, I didn't include other south shore locations on the Cape, because any that might exist would do so in the milieu of better opportunities on the major beaches and Cape Cod Canal. Why fish Bass River when you can have the Canal? Except for Hull Gut, the stretch from North River to Boston is fraught with problems that reflect the same hardening of access so common in and around cities. All the towns on the North River maintain a complicated system of parking stickers limited to residents. Plymouth's Duxbury Beach didn't survive the cut because of environmental considerations. The north bank of the Merrimack River mouth, which is Salisbury Beach, has a productive jetty, but it, too, is overwhelmed by Plum Island. Inside, along the Merrimack River, it is possible to wade and explore the marsh areas very close to the Badger Rocks, a well-known boat-fishing hot spot; next is "Butler's Toothpick," a popular navigation aid that keeps stripermen busy. This inner-river section is quiet enough to hear feeding gamefish at night, and it is possible to wade the flats with small plugs or fly-fishing gear; there are no parking hassles, as the lot at Salisbury Beach State Reservation is open to anglers. In late spring, a good run of better-size stripers make their way up the Merrimack River chasing alewives. I have seen Lawrence anglers cashing in there, drifting the "herring" the same way they do in the Canal. But these spots just can't hold up against the Bay State's other offers.

A worthwhile feature that we can offer with the Bay State is that readers, even non-members, can call the Massachusetts Striped Bass Association hotline, (617) 395–1791, for a statewide rundown. Association high command can be reached live at Neponset Circle Fishing and Darts, (617) 436–9231.

75

Westport River Area
Westport, Massachusetts

BEST MONTHS TO FISH: May through November.

RECOMMENDED METHODS: Plugging, live bait, and fly fishing.

FISH YOU CAN EXPECT TO CATCH: Stripers and bluefish.

HOW TO GET THERE: East of Fall River on Route 195, pick up Route 88 south.

The Westport River area is a composite of several spots that seem to have been largely forgotten by the angling world. They are the Westport River, Horseneck Beach, Gooseberry Neck, and Allen's Pond.

About a mile before the shore, where the Route 88 bridge crosses the Westport River, there is a boat-launching ramp on the right. A canoe can be paddled upstream just minutes from that ramp to an island where stripers often gather in the deep night. This is a highly protected estuary where the only hazards are the strong currents of the river and the wake created by boat traffic. In late May and early June, I have taken a number of twentyish stripers there on dead alewives. Moreover, because of the riverine nature of the water here, it is an excellent spot to fly fish.

Between the bridge and the open coast, as you proceed down 88, you will notice on the right the dunes that flank Horseneck State Beach. Here you will find a veritable garden of bass-frequenting holes and bars stretching over 2 miles from the causeway to Gooseberry Island on the east, and to Cherry Point, which guards the mouth of the Westport River, on the west. Cherry Point is a great spot on either tide, but I believe the drop has a slight edge. Access problems, however, rear their heads at Horseneck. While there is a road along the river that leads to Cherry Point, it is blocked and parking is prohibited. Similarly, there is no after-hours parking at Horseneck State Beach, which has spacious parking areas for bathers during the day. Again, as is so much the case throughout the Striper Coast, the access problems are worse in summer. With an oversand vehicle, I have driven Horseneck Beach in late fall when nobody cares. Horseneck Beach is one of those out-of-the-way spots that is largely forgotten.

Gooseberry Neck, at the east end of Horseneck, reaches seaward, forming a natural barrier. At the sou'west corner of Gooseberry, low tide, there is a nice mix of sandy bottom and rocky shore where stripers and blues seem always to gather. As you look west, you quickly realize that anything moving along the shore has to round this spot on its way to the Cape and islands. And, as is so often the case, positive influences can combine to make a great spot phenomenal. When you add an onshore sou'west—the prevailing summer wind—to a setting sun or rising moon and low tide, the results can be explosive. As this is state property, the only access problem is driving, because the causeway is blocked some years, or damaged by storms, forcing anglers to walk in.

If you go east where Route 88 bumps the shoreline, the shore road soon heads back inland. To the east, you'll see a collection of summer cottages that influence parking and access to Allen's Pond, which is owned by someone who lives elsewhere. You'll see an estuarine backwater that fills and empties with the sea. The opening to this pond lures gamefish all season. The difficulty of access to Allen's Pond varies from time to time.

Back at the mouth of the Westport River, the Acoaxet Rocks guard the west bank of the river entrance. From these rocks, one can easily see Cherry Point and Horseneck Beach a few hundred yards away, but to drive around the west branch of the river by road is 14 miles. Still, during the off-season for tourism, when locals are not around to complain about your parking, that west side of the river opening can host some Moby stripers. My first 50-pound-plus lineside was taken there.

CONTACT TIP: Call Westport Marine, (508) 636–8100, for information.

76

South Cape Beach/Waquoit Bay
Mashpee, Massachusetts

BEST MONTHS TO FISH: Late April and early May.

RECOMMENDED METHODS: Sea worms on the bottom and fly fishing.

FISH YOU CAN EXPECT TO CATCH: Stripers and blackfish (tautog).

HOW TO GET THERE: From Route 28 in Mashpee, turn south onto Great Oak Road and follow the signs to the New Seabury development.

At land's end, there is a parking area from which you can access South Cape Beach to the right (west) or Popponessett Beach to the east. Here, with a small piece of sea worm fished on the bottom with a light sinker in late April—say the twenty-seventh, give or take a day—you can usually catch the first schoolies of the season in great numbers. If you hook something that takes line from your drag, it is likely a blackfish, of which there are many at this time. About a mile west, there is a pair of jetties guarding the opening to Waquoit Bay, an estuary that is responsible for much of the appeal of this area.

An approach that used to be reliable—and most likely still is—is to wade into the bay in the back from the east bank of the jetty and cast eels into the current of an incoming tide. Unlike the front beach in spring, this is for larger bass all through the summer. The eel is tossed slightly upcurrent and allowed to drift inland, into the bay.

No doubt, the same technique will work, with similar results, in nearby Cotuit Inlet, to the east. But watch for boat traffic, which is greater here and could be a complication in summer. And I am certain there can be moderate fishing on Oregon Beach, which is just east.

With better choices available, I have not had the pleasure of working the more accessible inlets, such as the opening to Coon-amessett Estuary in Falmouth, or Bass River, a name that immediately makes the spot worth investigating. These places, unless you happen to be lodging locally and have a chance to establish yourself socially, are not likely to serve your needs when you consider the tendency of officials here to run outsiders off.

TIP: Make sure that the backing has greater strength than your strongest leader.

77

Nauset Beach
Orleans, Cape Cod, Massachusetts

BEST MONTHS TO FISH: Late May through October.
RECOMMENDED METHODS: Bottom fishing with sea worms, plug fishing, live eels, and fly fishing.

FISH YOU CAN EXPECT TO CATCH: Stripers and bluefish.

HOW TO GET THERE: Follow the signs on Route 28 in Orleans to Nauset Beach in East Orleans. (Oversand vehicle required.)

Nauset Beach is the most beautiful and primitive beach on the entire Striper Coast. The primordial beauty is only enhanced by the bars, sloughs, and holes you'll find the full length of the shore, stretching south until Pleasant Bay unfolds into view to the west. Except for a few private cottages, there is little on this natural peninsula that is man-made.

Access is controlled at the north in the town of Orleans. Part way down the beach, you'll cross into the town of Chatham. As a result, the municipalities share in the management and policing of the beach. Except for the large, well-paved parking area at the Orleans end, there are no developed roads to the south. The only ap-

Nauset is one of the prettiest sandy beach spots on the Striper Coast. Stripers, too!

proach is by beach buggy or by boat across Pleasant Bay, the latter an unlikely option for anyone wanting to fish at night.

A permit is required for this beach, and it is necessary for your four-wheel-drive vehicle to pass inspection for suitable equipment. Permits are issued at the Orleans police station on Route 28. At this writing, the towns charge an annual fee plus daily fees.

The structure and condition of the beach is the sum total of the preceding months' weather. Consequently, in some seasons there is little structure to appeal to stripers, while in others, holes and ditches mark more hot spots than can be fished in a night. As a rule, the shallower holes are vacated at low tide, though linesides will return to them as soon as they have enough water. Deeper spots, of course, will hold fish the tide around. In the bigger holes, tide has less meaning, and at high tide, structure is obscure, impossible to read, and less confining for the linesides feeding there. Thus, while fish can be in, they can be anywhere. A good rule is that the more extreme the structure, the more likely it is to host fish. It is also important to treat each edge of a hole as a separate item. Often, bass will hang on the north or south edge because of how the water sweeps over. One has to test these places to determine how the bite is taking place.

One reliable hole where structure is most likely to build to productive levels regularly from year to year is Pochet Hole, which is at the first opening in the dune track going left, or east. This is only a mile south of the beach access where a non-four-wheel drive can be parked. A person could walk that distance and have private fishing along the way, free of vehicles, which are restricted to the back track, out of sight; moreover, their lights are not able to spook fish from the shallow wash.

While the favored method along the beach is plugging, there is excellent fishing on the bottom with sea worms. Most anglers fish two rods, spacing bait different distances from the shore.

It is also a good idea to keep an eye and ear trained upon Pleasant Bay, which is the back side, or west, of Nauset Beach. Bass love—*love*—to run the inlet in the deep of night, feeding all through the bay, then slipping quietly into one of the bay's holes or back to offshore bars. I say an ear because often you will hear them popping and slurping in the relative quiet of these protected waters. Great spot for the fly rod.

CONTACT TIP: To find out what locals are saying about Nauset Beach, call the Goose Hummock Shop, (508) 255–0455.

78

Chatham Inlet
Chatham, Cape Cod, Massachusetts

BEST MONTHS TO FISH: Late August through early November, depending on birds.

RECOMMENDED METHODS: Plug fishing, live eels, and fly fishing.

FISH YOU CAN EXPECT TO CATCH: Stripers and bluefish.

HOW TO GET THERE: Follow the signs on Route 28 in Orleans to Nauset Beach in East Orleans. Drive the 8 miles south over sand to land's end. (Oversand vehicle required.)

At the south end of the beach, you will find an inlet where up to 11 feet of water is exchanged with Pleasant Bay. Here you are on the north bank of the same inlet in number 79, which is 2 crow miles away but a 20-mile drive. What degrades this spot is closure during the bird nesting season—May through August. At that time the last mile of beach is banned from oversand recreational vehicle use. Otherwise Chatham Inlet would be without doubt the best plug fishing striper hot spot in this book. Remarkably similar to the

Chatham Inlet is a tough grind oversand, but the big stripers can be there.

old Chatham Inlet, which was 4 miles south before the beach broke through in '87, regulars here fish it largely the same way.

The best tides are evening tides, those that are high at 7:00, 8:00, or 9:00. In autumn, when days are shorter, even 6:00 P.M. high will host stripers. Expect fish to come through the inlet just before dark, often running through in pods far into the night. Another excellent time is when the inlet slacks, roughly two hours after high tide on the Boston tide chart. It seems that those bass that had taken up feeding positions, perhaps out of reach, now shift for the new, falling water, creating an additional flurry of activity. A good rule for this spot is that if nothing comes in during rising water, you're not likely to see much during a dropping tide. Conversely, good fishing on the rise usually produces equally well on the drop. I must advise you, however, that during a full or new moon—high tide at midnight—fishing is at its worst.

Popular methods are plug fishing, much of it with the Finnish genre of swimmer: Rebels, Red-fins, Nils-Masters, Bombers, and Mambo Minnows. With larger bass, you are safer with the bigger models; but if stripers of any size prove picky, use smaller swimmers of the same models tied direct. Stay in method harmony with other surfcasters by "plugging" your live eels. Forget bottom fishing here, as currents make holding impossible, and it is not nice to cross the other anglers. Flycasters should set up downtide and have a 20-pound leader. Floating lines are fine.

TIP: Have a few 3/0 or 4/0 size flies, with barbs intact, of your favorite pattern for that night when Moby linesides are around. Big stripers have big mouths.

79

Chatham Inlet/South Island
Chatham, Cape Cod, Massachusetts

BEST MONTHS TO FISH: Late May through early November.

RECOMMENDED METHODS: Plug fishing, live eels, chunks and fly fishing.

FISH YOU CAN EXPECT TO CATCH: Stripers and bluefish.

HOW TO GET THERE: Follow the signs on Route 28 in Chatham to Chatham Light. Park in the lot across the street from the Coast Guard station where the lighthouse is located. Walk down a well-maintained stairway to the beach and inlet.

This new hot spot was formed during a 1987 winter storm when the beach broke through to leave an island to the south. Later, "South Island," as it subsequently became known, filled in that part of Pleasant Bay that separated it from the mainland. Today it is possible to walk across the new sand to the south edge of Chatham inlet or even fish the east facing South Island beach. The same waters as number 78, it is necessary to treat this side as a separate location because of its unique legal and geographic limitations that are not in place at the Nauset Beach approach to Chatham Inlet. For example, not only is it not necessary to have a buggy here, it is not allowed. Secondly, this side of Chatham Inlet enjoys deeper water and, consequently, a greater flow. Many anglers feel that the surfcasting is better here, and all agree that it is certainly more accessible. The best tidal considerations here are different, too.

Plan for a low tide, which occurs during darkened hours, and expect to make contact with stripers one hour either side of low tide on the Boston chart. Extremely reliable and impossible to explain, these two hours are absolute. Once water slows up an hour after low, it is pretty much over. Of course there are exceptions, but ratings lower outside those hours. Regulars here cast a plug, Slug-Go, or live eel and let it swing in the current on a tight line. To avoid conflict, bottom dunkers like to get off to the side of the lure fishermen and wait with sinkered chunks of whatever baitfish has been in the area, be it bunker or mackerel. In July '94 Stu Jones of Madison, Connecticut, took a 57-pound striper here on a sunny afternoon with a chunk while playing with his kids on the beach. **TIP:** When the wind is east, fish bite the least.

80

Nauset Inlet
Orleans, Cape Cod, Massachusetts

BEST MONTHS TO FISH: May through October.

RECOMMENDED METHODS: Plug fishing and fly fishing.

FISH YOU CAN EXPECT TO CATCH: Stripers and bluefish.

HOW TO GET THERE: Follow the signs on Route 28 in Orleans to Nauset Beach in East Orleans. Walking: Go north (left) from the parking lot. Driving: Watch for a right turn about a mile down Nauset Heights Road. (Oversand vehicle helpful.)

One of the oldest arguments among the Cape's surf regulars deals with the relative merits of the Nauset and Chatham inlets. At first the similarities are compelling. As with Chatham Inlet, there is a large exchange of tide at Nauset Inlet, this time to Town Cove in

Orleans and Eastham. The same tide requirements are in place as with Chatham Inlet, and the same angling methods are in use. There are, however, many more bars and holes flanking both sides of the Nauset Inlet, particularly the south side, which I recommend. Stripers will often hole up in these nice spots all night long. At low tide, a surfcaster can wade to these places for some productive plug fishing; but keep in mind that once the tide turns, it is easy to get trapped on one of the higher spots out there, forcing a dangerous crossing well over your waders.

An excellent stretch of water lies just to the north of the Nauset Beach parking lot, an area that is both accessible on foot and free of vehicular traffic. Within ¼ mile, you can be fishing surf that is influenced by Nauset Inlet's changeable waters without the hassle of police complaints. Along with being most suitable for stripers, this structure is the only place on all of the Outer Cape where you will find large rocks in the surf.

The politics of Nauset Inlet are another of those access frustrations that greet surf fishers. Officials have kept outsiders from driving there for over twenty years with the hopelessly arbitrary regulation of maintaining the public right-of-way for residents only. While townies have quietly used an access to the north in Nauset Heights for years, the Orleans police have required a resident "R" sticker from anyone who hoped to drive in as a means of excluding outsiders; yet, as long as I have fished there, I've never known anyone from outside to be brought before the courts. While I can offer no legal advice, I have doubts that any town can define "public" with such a limited interpretation.

A worthwhile digression that might deserve some attention here is that many maps show the Nauset Beach area—from Nauset Inlet south, including Monomoy Island—to be under the jurisdiction of the Cape Cod National Seashore; this, however, is not the case. Federal budget limitations and a reluctance on the part of the towns to relinquish control of their beaches place that possibility in the distant future. At this writing, Nauset Beach is *not* part of the National Seashore Park.

Regulars watch all three of these Nauset beach locations—the beach and its flanking inlets at either end; they fish them similarly, expect no fishable numbers of bluefish until August, and opt for a warm, dry bed whenever the wind is east.

TIP: When fishing inlets, remember that water will still be going "out" while the water you are standing in gets deeper. Know when to quit.

81

Outer Cape
Cape Cod National Seashore
Truro/Wellfleet, Massachusetts

BEST MONTHS TO FISH: August through October.

RECOMMENDED METHODS: Plugs, rigged eels, live eels, and fly fishing.

FISH YOU CAN EXPECT TO CATCH: Stripers and bluefish.

HOW TO GET THERE: Going north to Provincetown on Route 6, watch for signs on the right to the various swim beaches.

From High Head clear to the Eastham side of Nauset Inlet, there is a 22-mile stretch of wild beach about which little is commonly known. Here, great bars stretch seaward like fingers; at the corners where they meet the beach, there are holes where baitfish gather. At some of the prominent points, depending on the tide, the sea claps up straight where waves collide; along some straight stretches of shore, there are trenches where Moby stripers will swim all night looking for something to eat.

At the north end of this magical stretch, Highland Light warns the shipping lanes of impending doom. South of that there is Balston, Newcomb Hollow, LeCount, and Nauset North Beach. It is here that modern-day salvagers have about finished plundering the gold bullion and coin of the *Widah,* a wreck of Spanish origin whose grave has lain just outside the striper bars for 300 years. Here, many of the Cape's great stripers and surfmen have met in battle. This stretch south of Highland Light was the private killing ground of the legendary striperman Arnold Lane, and it was for years Frank Daignault's best-kept secret. This stretch was also the site of much of my autobiography, *Twenty Years on the Cape: My Time as a Surfcaster.*

Parking areas at High Head, Head-of-the-Meadow, Newcomb Hollow, LeCount, and Nauset North Beach are closed at night, but permits for fishing/parking are available at the Visitor's Center on Airport Road in Provincetown. On foot, it is possible to hike in to areas that you've scouted during the day. However, it is imperative that you minimize equipment to enhance mobility: Fish barefoot in summer; use only one rod; have a rope for no more than one fish; keep the plug bag small. Humongous stripers are here.

This is an area where access on foot must be chosen carefully. Many of the dunes are so high, so amorphous, that a person could be buried alive in a descent. Such incidents have been documented. Climbing such dunes in departure is also impossible. Fishing productivity would be enhanced with a beach vehicle, but that has not been allowed since the mid-1980s, when complaints from local pressure groups caused the entire stretch in this listing to be closed to vehicular traffic. On foot, a well-conditioned person could not sample 5 percent of the structure.

Years when it could be driven—the same years when I was a rod-and-reel commercial fisherman—my wife, Joyce, and I fished every hole, every slough, every bar. We had thousand-dollar nights back when people worked a month for that. No more. But those who can take the demands of this fine stretch of shore will find it worth the effort.

At this writing, the Park Service has been holding hearings (one at which I testified as a historical witness) in the matter of reopening this section of the Cape to vehicular use. It is, of course, the only feasible way to fish the vastness of the area. I can make no prediction at this time on the proposal's chances.

TIP: Stripers that have either been rooting for sand eels or sea worms will often have abrasions on their chin and lips from the sand.

82

Provincelands (Back Beach)
Cape Cod National Seashore
North Truro/Provincetown, Massachusetts

BEST MONTHS TO FISH: June through October.

RECOMMENDED METHODS: Plugs and rigged eels and fly fishing.

FISH YOU CAN EXPECT TO CATCH: Stripers and bluefish.

HOW TO GET THERE: Follow Route 6 into Provincetown, then take a right onto Race Point Road. Go right (east) at the ranger station when going on the beach. (Oversand vehicle necessary.)

Provincetown is four-wheel-drive country, and an oversand vehicle permit is required. As with Nauset, you'll need the proper oversand vehicle equipment to qualify. There are, however, no daily fees in addition to the cost of the season pass.

East of the ranger station, the sandy beach curves so slowly that a compass is needed to ascertain that you are moving in a circle. On that circle is a continuous series of points stretching 6 miles to High Head, the limit for utilization of oversand vehicles under present regulations. Each of these points, but particularly the first ones, the ones to the west, have traditionally been fished during the late half of the rising tide; however, my experience has been that you could catch great stripers in this area without regard to tide. Moreover, it has always seemed to me that the stripers on the Back Beach were larger than those at the Race.

Waters moving into and out of Cape Cod Bay can be felt all through this stretch, which approaches the tip of the Cape. Curi-

When the bluefish show, the whole gang turns out to plug the beach.

ously, currents are left to right most of the time at most places regardless of tide. Locals explain it as "back eddying," when water seems to be traveling in any direction that it shouldn't. As a result, best wind for this area is sou'west, and the harder the better, because the wind combines with the natural rips to make the water pull, which the fish like. What everybody does is travel from one point to another because such spots have shallow fingers of sand where bass and blues can lie downtide in depths to ambush what comes over. Surf fishers like to cast just a few points downtide of straight out and allow their swimmer to drum in the current while it swings. Once they no longer feel the tension, they rush their retrieve in for another cast and swing.

One of the things that enabled me to wreak havoc upon linesides for the many years that I lived and fished here was our refusal to accept the timing methods that traditional surfcasters used. While it is a slight break from tradition, I would advise working this area during the late part of the falling tide, the low, and even the rise, if fishing is holding up. During these periods, you will get a chance to see the structure of the beach and store information about where you should be fishing when the water is high.

Similarly, the early part of an east or southeast wind, down the beach from the right, can crank linesides up into a frenzy. But it is a question of intensity and timing: Once the easterlies get to pumping strong, the water dirties up and becomes no longer fishable. Moreover, there is a red weed, or mung, that gathers so thick in the surf at the more easterly end of this stretch that you can't even fish there most of the time. Once it goes east, this gunk spreads throughout the whole area and it is time to sack in.

These Provincelands are the storied shores where much of surfcasting tradition was born and where the old ways live on. For instance, it is the last stronghold of the conventional or revolving spool reel. Braided line of strong tests (45/50) is used here, and because of this equipment, the demand for humongous plugs, particularly swimmers, persists. Giant Pikies, Danny's, Atom 40's, Goo-goo Eyes, the GTS-3, the Reverse Atom, all stuff hard to find in today's tackle shops, are standard weaponry in P-town. You need such big plugs in order to load the pool cue rods and mighty reels. Keep in mind that I am not talking about ancient history here; this is how it is now.

In July of '77, the year of the Great P-town Blitz, Joyce Daignault, that consummate surfcaster of the highest order, landed a 50-pound, 6-ounce monster for which she won the Governor's Cup. What a night! What a girl!

CONTACT TIP: For information on P-Town and the Lower Cape, call Nelson's, (508) 487–0034, on Race Point Road.

83

Race Point
Cape Cod National Seashore
Provincetown, Massachusetts

BEST MONTHS TO FISH: June through October.

RECOMMENDED METHODS: Plug fishing, rigged eels, sand eel baits, and fly fishing.

FISH YOU CAN EXPECT TO CATCH: Stripers and bluefish.

HOW TO GET THERE: Follow Route 6, then take a right onto Race Point Road. Turn left, or west, at the ranger station. (Oversand vehicle recommended.)

Race Point Light, which lies a little over a mile west of the ranger station entrance, is the most reliable hot spot in P-town. There have been periods when stripers were there around the clock, usually when there was a howling sou'west in your face. Thankfully, this is a prevailing wind, because it is almost a requirement for fishing the Race with any success. There have also been times, such as during an east storm, when the Race was hot during the late end of a rising tide. Along with those wind requirements, another safe rule is the good fishing at low tide. Timing-wise, whenever Race Bar was crowded during a dropping tide, fish usually arrived three and a half hours after Boston high tide on the tide chart. It was usually time to quit once the tide was two hours up. I often felt that stripers were still there but that the rising water had backed us up so far that I could no longer reach the positioned fish with my plug. Because the intensity of the fishing is dependent upon the intensity of the sou'west, be prepared for fishing into a gale—a time you would never want to miss. This means that you should select plugs for their castability rather than for their catchability. Getting hits can be aided by using teasers—usually a small fly or rubber lure in front of the plug.

Only a few hundred yards east of Race Bar are the Traps, where a tide rip forms during the early rise. Often, the very fish that were on Race Bar at low tide had moved to the Traps once rising water began to run. The Traps, however, are not as reliable as the Race.

No examination of this area would be complete without some discourse on Hatches Harbor. This small inlet just south of Race Bar will sometimes gather stripers in its falling waters, but usually after low tide on the chart, when water is still emptying from the pond. But as it is with the rest of this locale, the situation is dependent upon sand eels moving into the pond. The bowl-shaped curve of the beach between Race Bar and Hatches Harbor can serve as a feeding ground for all sizes of striper.

Once the tide is down four hours, you can cross the harbor on foot and fish as far south as you please into New Beach or Herring Cove (two names for the same place). There were times when there were more bass south of the estuary than above. For this entire area, the formula, in addition to low tide, has always been a hardy sou'west wind. Those without a buggy can get a permit to park overnight for fishing at New Beach and cash in on what I speak of here.

Although sand eels are the prevalent bait here, slim, smallish Finland plugs work best. Or, you can rig a castable Gibb's Swimmer as a casting weight for a teaser rig. Best teasers are either Red-Gills or white eel flies tied on a 3/0 hook. Wind permitting, this is an excellent place for fly fishing. And if the wind is a two-flag whole gale, you can heave a bank sinker as a casting weight instead of the plug. It is along this very shore that I learned to heave lead with flies above them when the sea was white.

The tendency to use fresh sand eels as a bait for fishing the bottom is fairly recent here. The center of activity for this has largely been Race Bar, since the Park Service closed Wood End, where bait fishing had been popular. Consequently, vehicles are often parked two and three deep, with anglers using extra rods and creating such a picket fence of equipment that stripers actually bump lines when they swim past, giving the false signal that a bait has been taken. Along with little room for passing fish, plugging a stretch of beach at Race Bar is often out of the question. But the outer edges—Traps to the east, Herring Cove to the south—remain plug water.

A quarter mile east of the Traps, at Race City, where you'll usually see a number of self-contained (camper) vehicles, there is a tide rip that forms west to east at high tide. "Second Rip" or "Telephone Pole Rip," as it is variously called, is a traditional hot spot for big stripers; they come from the east for the bait and the warm currents that fall from Cape Cod Bay. Best time for this spot is when there is a moon or spring tide pulling, as they produce the greatest exchange of water. Moreover, it helps to have a good sou'west pushing in the same direction to make the water move even harder. I have also found that in midsummer, when nights are short, a 1:00 or 2:00 A.M. high tide leaves enough time for the tide to still be pulling at dawn—that magical period when a dull fire is lighting off in the east and linesides are feedin' and movin' like the Boston girls had the towrope. Always expect a serious run of first bluefish in early August. Perhaps you've already noticed a

Provincetown surf itinerary emerging that lets you fish at any stage of the tide. Low tide: the Race; rising: the Traps; late rising: Back Beach; high tide to down three: Second Rip; last of the drop: back to the Race. Check out that rating!

TIP: Shave an ounce here or there from fly tackle, because gorilla weights will end your night of fly fishing prematurely.

When a whole lot of fish meet with a whole lot of surfcasters, they call it Race Point.

84

Pamet River

Truro, Massachusetts

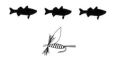

BEST MONTHS TO FISH: July through October.

RECOMMENDED METHODS: Plugging and fly fishing.

FISH YOU CAN EXPECT TO CATCH: Stripers and bluefish.

HOW TO GET THERE: From Route 6 in Truro, take Castle Road west to the end of Corn Hill Road; walk south along the beach to the river jetties.

Flanked by a pair of jetties, the Pamet River is a large estuary that reaches east into Truro from Cape Cod Bay. The north jetty of the opening is the best side for access. Here there is a parking area, and the walk over sand is only about 1/10 mile. As the largest estuarine inlet for 40 shore miles in either direction, the Pamet can have some good runs of bass at times. This spot has a reputation for producing more schoolies than monsters, but I should always be wary of such generalizations, because sooner or later the big fish do show up, as if only to dispute them.

As for timing and methods, you can find linesides in here at any time in season; but, as at any other spot, they are sometimes not around if there are no baitfish to lure them. Again, it is a case of sand eels or sperling imitations with the smaller plugs and light tackle. Even if it is blowing a gale, this is a great fly-rod spot, because you can sometimes have fish around and behind you. The tail end of the dropping tide is best.

TIP: Only amateurs think that you can't flycast on a windy night.

85

Sandy Neck Beach
Barnstable, Massachusetts

BEST MONTHS TO FISH: July through October.

RECOMMENDED METHODS: Plugging, sea worms, and fly fishing.

FISH YOU CAN EXPECT TO CATCH: Stripers, bluefish, and some sea-run brown trout.

HOW TO GET THERE: Traveling east on Route 6A, take a left onto Sandy Neck Road about 1½ miles after crossing Scorton Creek. (Oversand vehicle necessary.)

Sandy Neck is another of the Cape's oversand-vehicle beaches, this one managed by the town of Barnstable with permit regulations similar to those of other drivable beaches. Both ends of the 8-mile beach are flanked by inlets that can lure stripers. The east end has Barnstable Marsh and the west, Scorton Creek. The traditional method along this beach is to fish sea worms on the bottom. Naturally, at times, both inlets can provide some solid light-tackle fishing.

One of the problems with this area, despite its proximity to both the Canal and Cape Cod Bay, is that, as a north-facing beach, it does not often have a surf-favorable onshore wind. Among regular Cape stripermen who have fished the other beaches, Sandy Neck is the least popular. And, while boats in full view of the beach can tong all day long, it is often unaccountably deadsville. The horseflies alone are enough to make a surf fisher renounce this beach for all time.

Scorton Creek, which is at the beginning of the beach, hosts a unique fishery in the form of sea-run brown trout. Best fishing is fall and winter way up the creek during low tide. Use small lures or saltwater fly patterns for well-fed browns, which, though rare, can heft up to 5 pounds.

Brewster Flats

Because of their proximity to Sandy Neck, I feel compelled to mention the Brewster Flats, more as a warning than a numbered hot spot of the Striper Coast. The place is problematic, in that while it can be sensational fishing at times, it is among the most dangerous places you can fish for stripers. I have seen men cry in terror once they got turned around out there in a fog and rising tide. Problem is that this part of Cape Cod Bay is so shallow that it goes dry just long enough to invite an adventurous surfcaster—usually without a compass—onto its vast expanse. Within these flats, you can sometimes find Mr. Linesides trapped in a hole, feeding on sand eels, and you'll catch him when he has no place to run. Then, while putting your fish on a stringer, the water rises an inch and you can no longer tell which water is shallow and which is deep. Worse, what if you drop your flashlight?

The natural limitations of the Brewster Flats, combined with the limited parking opportunities and occasional police hassles, should be enough to make you reassess your priorities. I have lain in my bunk all day waiting for darkness and tide to fish there, and then wondered what it was about this spot that kept me from getting the sleep I needed so badly.

Best fishing is midsummer, and tell the Nickerson Funeral Home that Frank Daignault sent you.

TIP: When driving on beach sand, lower tire pressure so that the tires appear to be going flat. Roughly 10 psi on the average sport utility.

those reading water, it is possible to drive the shoreline scenic route around Cape Ann through Gloucester and Rockport. Keep in mind that this east-facing shore is impossible during major storms.

CONTACT TIP: Pete's Bait and Tackle in Salem maintains a hotline, (508) 744–2262, on exactly what is happening here.

88

Plum Island
Newburyport, Massachusetts

BEST MONTHS TO FISH: May through October.

RECOMMENDED METHODS: Sea worms, plug fishing, chunks, jigs, and fly fishing.

FISH YOU CAN EXPECT TO CATCH: Stripers, bluefish, winter flounder, and yellowtail flounder.

HOW TO GET THERE: From Route 1A Newburyport, follow the signs to Plum Island; this leads to Plum Island Boulevard, which is the only access road from Newburyport to the island.

Plum Island is nothing other than a 7-mile sandbar formed by the eons of flow from the Merrimac River. Most of the surf fishing takes place at the north end, the river end, which is served by a spacious parking area. Here you will find regulars gathered at the jetty to the east and at a sandbar to the north and west: The two spots are just under a mile apart. Weekends, when the fish are in, you can walk the shore and see countless lanterns glowing in both directions, marking the banks of the river.

The rule is that the river mouth (or "Point"), including the jetty

and bar, is best during the dropping tide. During the rise, many prefer the front beach, which is south of the breakwater. Hands down, the most popular striper bait is sea worms on the bottom. Along with traditional worm-fishing methods, Plum Island regulars of late "work the worms" in river currents, which is a system of casting egg sinkers above a swivel and leader that leads to a 5/0 to 7/0 baitholder claw hook draped with sea worms. This very effective bottom-bouncing technique is not likely to be seen elsewhere.

In early spring, about the first week in May, when the first small stripers usually arrive, jigs have become popular. Later in the month, plug fishing starts, along with an intensifying interest in fly fishing the river. In recent years, there have been runs of flounder—late May, early June—that are taken with worms on smaller hooks. Some of this is incidental to striper fishing, but the '92 flounder were so numerous that much of the fishing was directed toward them. Expect bluefish arrivals by early August. By then, chunks—either menhaden or mackerel—can be used for baitfishing. Striper purists who want their bait to cull blues out stick with worms. All fishing is usually over by October 15, but strays have been taken as late as early November.

A little more than 5 miles of the south end of Plum Island may be traversed by oversand vehicles. But these days, thanks to the same piping plovers that have closed other fishing beaches, no driving is allowed until August 1. Then, nightly permits are issued along with "self-contained" permits for those appropriately equipped. Roughly the same equipment and procedural requirements for beach-buggy use are in place here as elsewhere.

Upriver, this side of Surfland, the Joppa Flats (just west of Woodbridge Island) are extremely popular with fly fishers who wade from the nearby seawall. Low tide is the focus of activity, but when it is good, regulars press the time element by wading out late in the drop and learn from experience when to get out during the rise.

Plum Island is to Massachusetts what Montauk is to New York.

CONTACT TIP: Kay Moulton's Surfland Bait and Tackle, (508) 462–4202, is information central for Plum Island.

NEW HAMPSHIRE

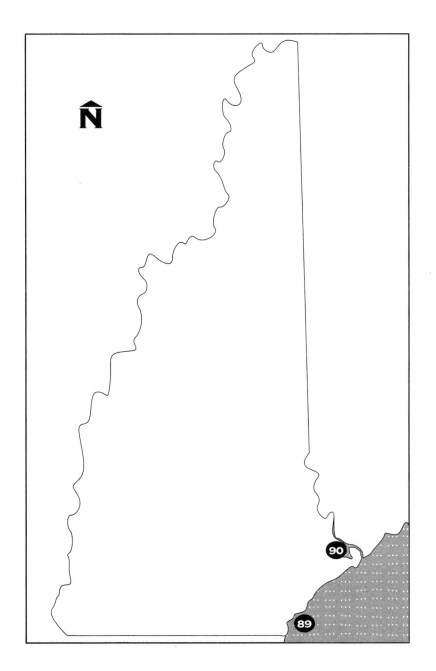

Gamefish observe no political boundaries and thus are bliss-
fully unaware that the short, 20-mile coastline they forage
between Massachusetts and Maine belongs to New
Hampshire. This segment of the Striper Coast is small, but it is
highly representative of the hydrology of nearby states. For its size,
New Hampshire rivals any of the other sections in terms of offer-
ing a savory mix of sand, stone, and estuary to lure gamefish.

In this book's preparation, I took into account all the demands
of anglers, geography, and natural opportunity; as a result, I could
only allow two hot spots from this state, knowing full well that
there are more. I have fought the numbers all through the preparation of this work, and New Hampshire sorely tested my shaky
ability to walk away from good fishing. Failing to survive the cut,
when it could have risen above many others anywhere else on the
coast, was Rye Harbor. I'm also certain that the Piscataqua Estuary
in Portsmouth—for all its industrial trappings—presents countless
shore-fishing opportunities of high order. Lastly, Great Bay hosts a
marvelous striper fishery all through the season, which no doubt
affords some good shore fishing for those willing to explore. The
hydrology of humping tidal exchanges is inspiring, and at these latitudes there are no summer doldrums.

89

Hampton River Inlet
Hampton, New Hampshire

BEST MONTHS TO FISH: Mid-May through early October.
RECOMMENDED METHODS: Plugs, live bait, and fly fishing.
FISH YOU CAN EXPECT TO CATCH: Stripers and bluefish.
HOW TO GET THERE: The Route 1A bridge in Hampton is just over the Massachusetts line on I–95.

This combination of estuary and oceanfront offers six distinct opportunities: sand beach, jetty, and back estuary on both sides of the river. The combination of beach, dunes, oceanfront, and estuary serves the needs of any level of fishing. The jetty offers a chance to reach the tide rips of the river, particularly on a falling tide. However, depending on the wind, these jetties are often wet, and they are always rough going, not to mention slick at low tide. Anglers commonly set up baited rods along the sandy beaches, using bunker or mackerel chunks or freshly dug sand eels. It is possible to walk the grassy shore in the back with a swimming plug after dark and locate feeding stripers by the sounds they make. Don't overlook the protected estuary as a great spot for fly fishing.

All of this is part of Hampton Beach State Park, where ample parking on both sides is never a problem during the night or early morning hours when you should be fishing. Keep in mind, however, that it is illegal to fish the bridge here. Also, the arrival and departure of bathers during the day in summer—fantastic crowds at both Hampton and Salisbury—unleash rapidly snarling traffic that can trap any unsuspecting fisherman. In late afternoon, or during a sudden shower, the entire world tries to leave all at once.

TIP: Like other surf methods, fly fishing for stripers works best at night.

90

General Sullivan Bridge
Great Bay
Portsmouth, New Hampshire

BEST MONTHS TO FISH: June through September.

RECOMMENDED METHODS: Alewives, sea worms, eels, pogies or bunkers, and bucktail jigs.

FISH YOU CAN EXPECT TO CATCH: Stripers.

HOW TO GET THERE: From either direction on Route 95 in Portsmouth, take the Spaulding Turnpike north toward Newington and Dover. After going over the first bridge, about 3 miles from 95, take routes 16 and 4 and exit north toward Dover. This turn will lead to parking facilities that are at either end of the General Sullivan Bridge.

Replaced by a larger, more modern span, the roughly 500-foot-long Sullivan Bridge is now a state-managed fishing site—no traffic. Equally important is the fact that this is where the Piscataqua and Little Bay come together. Taking tidal exchange into account, one soon realizes that massive currents mingle in this area to provide ample foraging opportunities. At slack tide, however, stripers—BIG stripers—play a game of musical chairs as they shift positions with changes in the water. Regulars make it a point to be at the bridge when the tide slacks (really less than an hour), to take advantage of moving linesides. Otherwise, full tides of 6 or 8 knots make fishing tough.

I rate this spot high because its potential for a real brute of a striper is matched by few other spots in this territory. Big live baits supported by heavy tackle are in order here. This is no place for a budding amateur to learn the ropes. For instance, it is possible to fish bucktail jigs when the water is speeding up at the eddies in front of bridge pilings to lengthen one's time of opportunity. And, depending on the light, you can sometimes see stripers in the bridge shadows, but they face the current and scoot for the bridge's underside after the hook is buried. With a humping tide, no usual strength of line is going to take the combined forces of tide and striper without blood, sweat, and tears at both ends. Better fishermen know how to stretch the time window and when to crank drags down against dangerous pilings, as well as how to deal effectively with heavy lines.

Some ten years ago, I fished this area from a boat with Dick Pinney, who was kind enough to share this spot with me. At that time, stripers having faded to a mere shadow of their former numbers, we sought coho salmon. Now that the stripers are back, that program has fallen by the wayside, but I learned two things then: that Great Bay is appropriately named, and that Pinney knew both its waters and stripers as well as anyone around.

CONTACT TIP: Sud's and Soda, (603) 431–6320, knows about the Sullivan Bridge.

MAINE

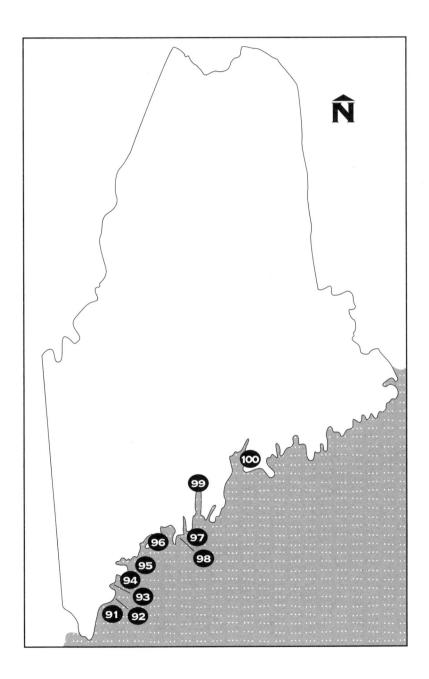

I have no doubt that one of the weaknesses of this book is its coverage of Maine. In my investigations of that state, I learned quickly that the magnitude of its coastline—when all the nooks and crannies are taken into account—is positively intimidating. It would have served no purpose to try to actually measure the shoreline, but I suspect there are more miles here than in all the other Striper Coast states combined. Therefore, it would not be unreasonable to say that I could easily find one hundred hot spots in its fjords alone. To do so, however, would not be in keeping with my object of providing a usable range of suitable surf-fishing locations in harmony with population needs. As it is, Maine already has more shore fishing that it can use, though the activity is not concentrated on the more southern coasts, as the forthcoming listing might imply. It is rather more evenly distributed, but I lean toward the south end because, since this book must have reasonable limits, I prefer to focus on spots where there are people to utilize them.

Maine's bountiful resources are further enhanced by the view its inhabitants take toward the enjoyment of the outdoors and access to it. In Maine, most landowners would not even look up from their newspapers to concern themselves with a passing sportfisher, unless it was to shout a friendly greeting. Conversely, in most of the states that make up the Striper Coast, shorelines are so jealously guarded that the discreet habits one must use to gain access, such as fishing in the deep of night and hiding one's auto, are as much a part of shore fishing as sharp hooks. Thus, not only does Maine have more, but its people—save for a few newcomers—are more anxious to share it.

Few would find fault with Maine's traditionally intense interest in sportfishing. Indeed, this bastion of outdoorsmanship is known worldwide for its fishing. On closer examination, however, one discovers that Maine's angling traditions *do not* include saltwater fishing, let alone surfcasting. Indeed, the usual characterization of Maine sportfishing is born of pristine mountain streams and placid lakes teeming with trout and salmon, not a raging surf with linesides darting through the foam. Thus, since both the above pictures are versions of the true Maine, the freshwater bias must be a social rather than natural phenomenon. It might be explained in either of two ways: Perhaps the sportfishers of Maine did not know what they had; or maybe trout and salmon adequately filled their needs. In any case, that is all changing.

Even Maine is beginning to feel the pinch of increased population and the commensurate pressures upon its resources. Traditional anglers find themselves packing and paddling in deeper and deeper each season to escape the crowds. At the same time, they are discovering astonishing fishing opportunities right in their own backyards and in the shadows of some larger cities like Augusta and Bangor. Some of them have to be asking themselves, "Why travel days to the Alligash for a 2-pound brook trout when there are 15-pound blues smoking your fly reel on your lunch hour?" Few will admit it, even to themselves, but the salt chuck is new fishing for most Mainers. One need only examine the skill levels in evidence to recognize that they've been fishing sweet water a lot longer.

Of course, there are pioneers in saltwater fishing there who are smart enough to smell the coffee of this state's coastal sportfishing potential. Walter Johnson, of Johnson Sporting Goods fame, could never be accused of snoozing in the shadow of mildewing "lobsta pots" after opening four stores, spread from Portland to Rockland—all on the coast and all specializing in saltwater bait and tackle. Another saltwater advocate is Cal Robinson of Saco Bay Tackle Company, who, in addition to spreading the news about shore fishing, has championed offshore fishing for big game species—something Maine seemed to know nothing about until recently.

Besides clean water, let's talk about a few things you won't see anywhere else. The tidal exchange, for anyone coming from below Cape Cod, is huge here at 12 feet in the south and increasing as one travels north. Talk about tide rips! On the other hand, fishing seasons are much shorter than those in, say, Montauk, starting nearly a month later in spring and ending October 15 instead of November

15. With hunting time at hand, it is time to end fishing, even if the fish are still biting. Mainers love their hunting. Lastly, I can't discuss seasons without emphasizing that Maine water temperatures should allay any fears one might have of summer doldrums. Indeed, July and August are the best months to be fishing here.

The cut list for Maine is considerable, but it is a mere fraction of what it could be. Many of the rejected venues easily deserve inclusion as numbered hot spots: Long Beach at York, untold shore stretches on the Kennebec River above Fort Popham, and Reid State Park on Georgetown Island only scratch the surface. Every salmon river in Maine is a suitable striper river. In fact, there are probably more bass caught by salmon fishers—thinking they've just hooked the fish of their dreams—than by those who are really striper fishing. It happens on the Saint Croix River all the time.

91
Mousam River
Kennebunkport, Maine

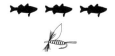

BEST MONTHS TO FISH: June through October.

RECOMMENDED METHODS: Plugs and fly fishing.

FISH YOU CAN EXPECT TO CATCH: Stripers and bluefish.

HOW TO GET THERE: After using exit 2 of the Maine Turnpike (Route 95), drive Route 9 through Wells to Route 1. Proceed 2 miles north on Route 1, then go right (east) on Route 9 until you see signs on the right for Parsons Beach—about 2 miles.

The Mousam River is a perfect example of the value of estuaries as feeding spots for stripers and blues. This marvelous tidal marsh meanders for many miles inland before the water freshens. Meanwhile, these waters host numerous baitfish while emitting their scent seaward on a dropping tide. That is why regulars here prefer wading the flats on a falling tide in the deep of night, where sometimes Moby stripers can be found waiting in the currents of the river. Figure the last three hours of the drop in tide and keep in mind that water will still be dropping from the river long after the ocean front has begun to rise.

According to my experience, when access and size are taken into account, the Mousam is the best of them, but similar local estuaries like the Webhannet River to the south and a few others above could provide yet unmeasured opportunities.

CONTACT TIP: Eldredge Bros. Fly Shop, (207) 363–2004, in Cape Neddick knows about the Mousam River fishing.

92

Saco River
Biddeford/Saco, Maine

BEST MONTHS TO FISH: June through October.

RECOMMENDED METHODS: Lures and baits.

FISH YOU CAN EXPECT TO CATCH: Stripers and bluefish.

HOW TO GET THERE: From exit 4 of the Maine Turnpike (Route 95), pick up Route 111 east into Biddeford to Route 1.

The Saco River is one of the classic striper and bluefish hot spots in the state. A certain care must be taken in this claim, however, because the reputation was gained largely from boat fishing; otherwise, I would sing its praises even higher. Still, there are any number of hot spots used by surfcasters that can be combined here riverwide.

The Camp Ellis Jetty on the north bank, the Saco side, reaches out into the open Atlantic at the Saco River's mouth. Casts on the south side of this north breakwater would take advantage of falling river currents. In fall, I would check the point where rocks meet the shore on the north side during a north or nor'west wind, as bait and migrating gamefish might tend to gather there.

With plenty of fish in the river, the "Meadow," which is half a mile short of Camp Ellis, is both a protected and productive spot in the river. You'll recognize the Meadow, because it is where the road comes closest to the Ferry Road leading to Camp Ellis. Swimming plugs in the deep night are fine, but if you are a fly rodder, you'll get good results here.

Salmon fishers are sometimes bothered by June stripers at the saltwater barrier of Cataract Dam. You can find this spot from the nearby bridge by looking upstream for the locally famous all-night eatery called Rapid Ray's.

On the south bank, or Biddeford side, some of the locals fish the "Gazebo" behind New England College. Another mile east, at Hills Beach, you'll find the Biddeford Pool, a mile-wide round chamber of salt water; it forms an incredible tide rip during the falling tide. Billy Gardner, my confidant and chief adviser on matters pertaining to Maine, says the Biddeford Pool is a much-overlooked local hot spot. Mush north—"On, you huskies!"

CONTACT TIP: Facts and equipment are available from Saco Bay Tackle Co., (207) 284–4453.

93
Old Orchard Beach
Maine

BEST MONTHS TO FISH: July through October.

RECOMMENDED METHODS: Lures, plugs, cut bait, and live eels.

FISH YOU CAN EXPECT TO CATCH: Stripers and bluefish.

HOW TO GET THERE: From any point on Route 1 in Saco, it is possible to follow signs to the Route 9 shore road of Old Orchard.

My old friend John Fleury loves to tell about how the Quebec Frenchmen will show up each season to bathe in the relatively tepid waters of the Gulf of Maine at Old Orchard and invariably end up blitzing bluefish on the sandy beach there. Because this meeting of man and fish is unplanned, it can satisfy any regular's entrepreneurial spirit, as well as his sense of social responsibility, to put surf rods in the anxious hands of the Quebecois—at a rate of ten bucks per fish. Thus, it is possible at times to stroll the sands of Old Orchard, a stack of surf rods on one's shoulder, and end up stowing a bundle of folding green. Many a great bluefish and excited tourist have met under such conditions, the latter crying, "*Mon dieu!*" as he marveled at his success. But I am supposed to be telling you more about how *you* can do this.

It is a little over 6 miles from the Camp Ellis breakwater to the Pine Point limit at the mouth of the Scarborough River. At any point along this vast stretch of greater Old Orchard, it is possible to

The best Old Orchard surfcasting is at night or days in the fall.

locate stripers and blues. Naturally, all traditional methods work, but a chunk of mackerel or bunker anchored to the bottom with a fishfinder rig is popular. Also, many Mainers like to fish a live eel along stretches of open beach like this one. During the day in summer, it is not advisable to wrangle with bathers; the nights, however, are quiet, desolate really. Seawater temperatures being what they are here, no conflict is likely in fall. If the tide happens to be dropping, the small inlet at Ocean Park (still Old Orchard) offers an attractive tide rip with waters warmed by the daylight sun that might have the bait to draw gamefish. This estuary is the only break in the straight shore and is a must visit during a night of fishing.

TIP: When fishing inlets, remember that tide lags and usually changes later than those times listed on the chart.

94

Scarborough River Marsh
Scarborough, Maine

BEST MONTHS TO FISH: June through October.

RECOMMENDED METHODS: Plugs, live eels, and fly fishing.

FISH YOU CAN EXPECT TO CATCH: Stripers and bluefish.

HOW TO GET THERE: From Route 1 in West Scarborough, take Pine Point Road east for 3 miles to a bridge over the railroad tracks. Then take a right into the yard of Snow's Canning Factory and follow it around underneath the road beside the tracks. Follow the railroad tracks north on a parallel road for less than 1 mile to another trestle over the river and its marsh.

This is one of those out-of-the-way spots where only locals go that can produce some truly religious striper opportunities. The marsh is a wild and unfettered natural setting comprising miles of estuarine grasslands and swamp. Loaded with bait hidey-holes, it is fed by numerous sweet-water streams that host anadromous baitfish. It is something that all good stripers know enough to look for.

Because this marshland almost totally drains with the tide, it is best to fish the late rise in water and the early drop—a total of five hours. Again, the locally prevalent bait is best, and these days it is usually menhaden. Regulars drift dead baits or chunks into the tide from the trestle. In June, when sea worms are hatching out, these could be drifted live-line with clinch-on or split-shot combinations to achieve the right level for feeding stripers. Keep in mind, however, that bluefish, once they arrive, don't show much interest in worms. Some striper purists take advantage of this specifically to keep blues away.

TIP: The Boston tide chart, with only a few minutes of adjustment, is okay to use in Maine.

95

Spurwink River
Higgins Beach, Maine

BEST MONTHS TO FISH: June through October.

RECOMMENDED METHODS: Plugs, eels, and flies.

FISH YOU CAN EXPECT TO CATCH: Stripers and bluefish.

HOW TO GET THERE: From Route 1, take Route 207 east; at

Route 77 (which is also Spurwink Road), turn left and continue to the right turn onto Ocean Avenue at the Higgins
Beach sign. Park across the street from the grocery store.

The mouth of the Spurwink is about a ½-mile walk north of the
small grocery store on the main road into the seaside village. Parking is available here for a nominal fee during the day and free at
night. No public parking is available at the beach.

Where the south edge of the river meets with open water, testy
collisions of tide flow and surf occur. Night stripers gather in this

*A combination of river and open surf, the mouth of the Spurwink River is
popular with flycasters for stripers and blues.*

sandy section, and surfcasters equipped with waders follow the shallows of a receding tide. The late drop is better, and in order to have this take place during the hours of darkness, high tides of 6:00, 7:00, or 8:00 P.M. are best. You'll often see or hear working fish in the tide rips of your foreground. In the outlet channel, up from the surf, fly fishing can be practiced in comfort, but there are fewer bluefish, as they prefer more open water. To the right of the inlet, clear of the river currents, there are a number of holes that often hold stripers (they change year to year). It is possible to fish bait here, but most of the Spurwink regulars plug, and their favorite time is when the tide is rising again.

CONTACT TIP: From Casco Bay to the Kennebec River, Barnes Outfitters, (207) 772–4222, in Portland, is a full outfitter with six guides.

96

Martin Point Bridge
Presumpscot River
Portland, Maine

BEST MONTHS TO FISH: June through October.

RECOMMENDED METHODS: Live pogies or mackerel (whole or chunks).

FISH YOU CAN EXPECT TO CATCH: Bluefish and stripers.

HOW TO GET THERE: Take exit 9 from Route 295 to Route 1. The nearby railroad trestle can be approached via parking areas at either end.

I say blues and stripers in that order, because, when summer action peaks, it's usually with great numbers of bluefish. In spring and fall, it can be stripers, but I saw the spot in early August at a time when every person who had ever hankered for a fish was drifting bait in the rips below the trestle. Crowds were so great that many of the serious locals had devised methods of taking their fish straight up instead of leading them past other anglers to shore. Live pogies or chunks are used, and three hours either side of high tide is favored.

A similar situation exists at the nearby B&M Railroad trestle that guards the opening to Back Cove (get off Route 295 at exit 8). Tidal exchange is not as great, but some locals come here to escape the crowds at Martin Point.

TIP: Neoprene waders are both warmer and more buoyant than those made of other materials.

97
Popham Beach
Phippsburg, Maine

BEST MONTHS TO FISH: June through October, but especially July.

RECOMMENDED METHODS: Plugs, chunk baits, and fly fishing.

FISH YOU CAN EXPECT TO CATCH: Stripers, bluefish, and occasional mackerel.

HOW TO GET THERE: Take Route 209 south from Route 1 in Bath and stay on it to land's end at Fort Popham—about 18 miles.

It is a short walk from the ample parking at Fort Popham State Park to the sandy shoreline that is also the mouth of the Kennebec River. Because of the river, there are powerful tide rips here developed by the huge upstream fjord of the Kennebec. As one walks south, or seaward, the currents of the river subside, and the seascape takes on the appearance of a more natural sandy beach. Because of the influence of the river, the area nearly always hosts somewhere between good and amazing numbers of stripers or blues or both. Weekend nights in summer, you can often see the

Popham Beach is turning Maine into a saltwater fishing state.

lanterns of anglers stretching south and west with the bend of the beach, waiting for a gamester to come along and take a piece of menhaden or mackerel. They bury sand spikes deep for good reason. Nearer to the fort, where the currents are greatest but the surf lighter, people are inclined to plug. This is also a suitable spot for fly fishing, and, considering the depths (Bath Iron Works launches cruisers into this river), fast-sinking fly lines are advised for best results. The best fishing is the closest, but there are 2 miles of beach for those with a hunter's spirit.

CONTACT TIP: The Brunswick store of Johnson's Sporting Goods, (207) 725–7531, knows the status of Popham Beach.

98
Morse River
Phippsburg, Maine

BEST MONTHS TO FISH: July through October.
RECOMMENDED METHODS: Plugs and fly fishing.
FISH YOU CAN EXPECT TO CATCH: Stripers and bluefish.
HOW TO GET THERE: From Route 1 in Bath, take Route 209 south, following signs to Popham Beach State Park.

A dune trail from the parking area leads to the sandy shore. Walking right, or southwest, for ½ mile will bring you to the Morse River estuary. This is the gateway to the popular boat-fishing spot for bass and blues called Spirit Pond. Less well known is the fact that surfcasters can walk the flats here at night, whether with plugs or fly fishing, and find excellent numbers of cruising stripers that often betray their presence by slapping bait wildly.

While it is possible to wade nearly all through here safely, the key to doing it right is to operate during the tail end of a dropping tide, but listen to your fears: Get out quickly once the tide starts rising! A no doubt friendly dispute rages among local stripermen as to which is Maine's best, the Morse River or Fort Popham.

TIP: It is widely believed that fifty degrees is the temperature at which stripers do not feed.

99

Kennebec River

Augusta, Maine

BEST MONTHS TO FISH: June and July.

RECOMMENDED METHODS: Fly fishing, plugs, and jigs.

FISH YOU CAN EXPECT TO CATCH: Stripers and Atlantic salmon.

HOW TO GET THERE: From I–95, take Western Avenue (exit 30) for 1½ miles east to State Street (Route 27). About a mile north on State Street, take a right onto Bond Street and drive down to the river. There is public parking behind the Eagles hall.

Below the dam in Augusta, stripers of up to 20 pounds show early each June and stay until early July. Fishing here is really freshwater, if tasting it is the criterion. By law, however, the river is considered tidewater below the dam, so no freshwater fishing license is required. This fishery is composed of mostly undersize school stripers, the source of which remains unknown. Because the Kennebec has its own nonmigratory population of stripers and is known to be visited by migratory bass as well, the fish you'll experience here are no doubt a combination of both groups.

The great numbers of stripers here were discovered in the late seventies by salmon fishers who gather on the river banks each June, particularly at the mouth of Bond Brook. While the Kennebec is not managed as a salmon river, insofar as there are great numbers of juvenile stock-outs, hundreds of Atlantics show up each spring. Fishery managers theorize that these salmon probably were released in the nearby Penobscot and have mistakenly returned to the wrong river—an anomaly of salmon behavior that is not all that uncommon and that encourages the natural distribution of their population. Similarly, brown trout are often caught here on an incidental basis. I point this out to explain why stripermen sometimes catch salmon, and why salmon fishermen often—much to their dismay—catch stripers. Incidentally, if you are serious about salmon fishing, your methods must be limited to fly fishing, and you must have a salmon license even in tidewater.

TIP: A 50-pound striped bass is between twenty and twenty-five years old.

100
Penobscot River
Bucksport to Bangor, Maine

BEST MONTHS TO FISH: June and September.
RECOMMENDED METHODS: Fly fishing and plugs.

FISH YOU CAN EXPECT TO CATCH: Stripers and Atlantic salmon.

HOW TO GET THERE: Take Route 1A south from Bangor to Prospect Street, then east on Route 174 to the Bucksport Bridge, which leads to Verona Island. Just before the next bridge, take a left to a public boat-launching ramp where locals fish in view of Bucksport, which is across the river.

This tidewater section of the Penobscot River is split by Verona Island. The narrowest side, called East Channel, which is an easy-to-use rocky shore, presents the best tide rips, particularly during a falling tide. The spot is popular enough to attract a steady level of visitation. Folklore puts the best fish seen here around the low forties. The Bucksport/Verona Island shoreline is fjord-like conifer forest and largely undeveloped. Stripers can be found on any part of Penobscot Bay, but this is one of the more reliable and accessible locations.

I first learned of the striper opportunities here while salmon fishing 25 miles upstream in Bangor at the Bangor Salmon Pool. It is a popular spot for schoolie fishing by the mid-June arrival time. This brackish area has a distinct tide and entertains linesides all day and night. Upstream a mile, beneath the Veazie Dam and clear of ocean influence, salmon fishers catch small striped bass incidental to their business. Again, as with the Kennebec (hot spot number 99), no license is needed for linesides, but a salmon license and fly fishing are requirements for salmon.

At Veazie, the best fishing is for Atlantic salmon, which begins May 1 but doesn't really get going until the first June runs of sea-run salmon. In its eighties glory days, the Penobscot provided an annual return of 3,000 to 6,000 mature fish, which were the results of a half million or more juvenile stock out. Now a mere handful of hangers-on fish for what little natural reproduction took place that survived the high seas nets—only a few hundred 4- to 16-pounders per season.

CONTACT TIP: Van Raymond Outfitters, (207) 989–6001, in Brewer is likely to know more about the Penobscot.

USING YOUR HEAD
TO GAIN ACCESS

One of the reasons why surfcasting does not enjoy the popularity of boat fishing is that access to the shore can be an interminable nightmare. Before long, the serious surfcaster realizes the truth: he is not wanted at the shore. No kidding.

After gaining permission to park, you can walk a public beach to be attacked by a 90-pound Lab that rips the waders off you. After a successful night of fishing, exhausted from lack of sleep and the night-long bullying of a relentless surf, you drag yourself—and a fish—back to your car to find that it has been towed. And you, certain that it presented no problem to anyone at that hour, know that the tow-truck operator isn't going to give it back until you hand over a day's pay in towing and storage charges that will be split between him and the police officer who called him.

Here in the Northeast, there are places where deeds, first drawn and granted by a king, extend out to sea a specified yardage past the *low*-water mark, where it would take a diver to drive a stake and where even a passing boat could be cited for trespassing. I know of a spot in Westport, Massachusetts, where somebody was shot and killed for refusing to leave such a place. And, while I could cite numerous examples, I think I have made enough of the lengths to which coastal dwellers will go to retain control not only over that which they own, but over all that they can see. The truth is that coastal habitation is fraught with distrust for outsiders, and, once you have had some exposure, a pattern of conspiracy emerges in which entire societies seek to exclude all others with the help of their police.

Indeed, any place where the law fails to accomplish this purpose, other means are quickly devised to serve the ultimate goal of "exclusivity." So-called public rights-of-way are grown over with rustic-looking ivy or blocked with stones; often signs that might have indicated an access to the shore are mysteriously "missing." Frequently, local governments work closely with landowners to make certain that anyone with a place to park has no place to walk, and vice versa.

There is also something inherently evil about the night—the very time when surfcasting is best practiced. Unaccountably, as a culture we remain marvelously close to our witch-burning forebears. Anyone who is enthusiastic about nighttime pursuits is deemed evil, immoral, or at least up to no good. Thus, anyone fishing at night is stigmatized by a clear presumption of guilt. Let's face it: We have a seemingly insurmountable set of social and legal obstacles before us if we want to fish the beach.

How, then, are we to cope with this access situation if we mean to go on surfcasting? Use access regulation to our advantage.

Truck in water: There are regulations for beach use and failure to follow them can lead to hard times.

First, fish the deep of night in the more sensitive areas. Avoid movement during change of police shifts—usually midnight. Of course, hide your vehicle and be prepared to walk farther than normal in order to separate the two elements of parking and fishing, which the authorities have so inevitably linked in their minds. So often when fishing I have had police ask me where I was parked. I tell them I was dropped off.

In most cases, though not all, police officers are uneasy about hassling fishermen. They know—better than anyone—that the world is too full of miscreants and malefactors lurking in the shadows for them to be bothering some poor person who has worked all week and now wants no more than to enjoy a few hours of harmless fishing. As a result, it is often possible to appeal to a police officer's better side once he or she understands that you are fishing. This, of course, is dependent upon your behavior, your manner during any exchange, the officer's predisposition, and the extent of your transgression.

Drink always erects barriers. If you have a vehicle full of empties and a little of the stuff on your breath, you are going to be kicked out and then asked to take a Breathalyzer test 100 yards down the road.

Everyone is intimidated by a crowd, not just police. When you fish with five other people, enforcement tends to assert itself more. Conversely, a person who is alone is less of a threat, less likely to inspire resistance or confrontation.

All public beaches forbid sleeping in a vehicle. This is important information for surfcasters, who practice their craft at all hours. We all have experienced slow fishing on a night when the sandman was nudging. By tradition, a fellow sitting up wearing waders—even if his eyes are shut—is *resting;* but if his body falls during the onset of rapid eye movement, he is *sleeping.* Going horizontal can get you kicked out. Of course, surfcasters have an easier time keeping a low profile because of night fishing. Locals, whether they own the land or not, can't harass you if they themselves are sound asleep. Don't wake them with a beer party.

The level of sophistication in policing today dwarfs what was in evidence only a generation ago. I have vivid recollection of police threatening to lock people up for "being a smart aleck." Barrington, Rhode Island, used to enforce an ordinance against all street parking in the town. I recall late-night "routine checks" (since struck down by the Supreme Court) in which we—there were three of us, one an off-duty police officer—had to explain where we were going and what we were doing—with six surf rods on the roof! On Nauset Beach, as recently as ten years ago, a police officer would spend the night warning all drivers with New York tags that he would cite them for speeding if they didn't slow down; he never did this to anyone from Massachusetts. While this might explain my attitudes, at least in part, I hasten to add that such outrages today are less likely. What you'll get now is a more thought-out, better planned heave-ho.

Sometimes, it is possible to raise the stakes if (1) you are prepared to engage an attorney, or (2) you *are* an attorney. I was once ordered to remove my vehicle from an, ahem, "private road" by a police officer when I knew the town plowed it every time it snowed. I held my wrists out and told him to arrest me. He didn't, but what if he had? I have repeatedly been confronted with situations where I could have gone to court with representation and made fools of the local authorities. But is that the price you want to pay for a night of fishing? To a great extent, it's a bluffing game, and police dread having to go to court to defend their actions when they are as arbitrary and capricious as they sometimes seem. Of course, when the towns are bluffing it doesn't go that far, but it still spoils your night. And they only go on to do it to somebody else.

But don't overlook the fact that you may lack the legal judgment to pick the right situation for taking on the law. You could simply be wrong.

The impression that a discussion like this one tends to generate is that the beach is perpetually guarded by armed uniformed security forces dragged along the seascape by hungry, panting, razor-toothed guard dogs, but that is only true west of Montauk and at a progressively diminishing level east of there. Fact is, the farther up the Striper Coast one goes, the less validity there is to the notion that access is even a problem worth talking about. My old surfcasting friend Ken Hancock, a Connecticut native with a measure of striper blood in his veins, says, "It is impossible to be on the beach at night in this state unless you know someone with waterfront property." On the other hand, the Rhode Island shore presents a changing picture where hope for access begins to surface. This hope later flourishes (with certain notable federal exceptions on Cape Cod) to the point where you can fish the night naked without embarrassment by the time you get to the rockbound coast of Maine. Not only is there hope, there is surfcasting at any hour, with any number of rods, with any friend you might choose.

TEN COMMON
SURFCASTING ERRORS

1. Failure to fish at night, particularly for stripers.
2. Use of tackle that is too light.
3. Lack of suitable contingencies for landing a world-class striper. Unprepared.
4. Poor knots.
5. Hooks that are too large.
6. Dull hooks.
7. Failure to understand natural, environmental conditions and their interrelationships with fishing.
8. Listening to people speculate about where the fish are or what is happening when they don't have a clue.
9. Use of rancid or unfresh baits.
10. Failure to read the water.

PLACES IN TIME

The familiar feeling of thinking that I've said it all visits me at the close of each book. Having published my autobiography *(Twenty Years on the Cape: My Time as a Surfcaster)*, then *Striper Surf*, an extensive how-to book on surfcasting for stripers, and now a catalogue of the Striper Coast's best locations, I see time as the only subject left to treat.

We can all be thankful that this enigmatic last item remains as wild as the wind and the sands pushed about by it, because the magical relationship between time and place will never be uncovered nor understood. It would be a bad thing for fishing if it were. We all are victims of time, all served by it. We all are wise enough to save it. We are all experienced enough to recognize that each place we visit, for whatever purpose, is never the same on a different day. Time is the one thing that we will never fully understand, regardless of how well we fish or how well we choose our places. Time is too subjective, too fleeting, too different with each day that passes. But most of all, time was the thing I was once not smart enough to fear.

Time was when I worried about two things: I worried that we would lose our fish, and I lamented that soon we might have no place where we could try for them. Now, some thirty years later, we have as many fish as we've ever had in my lifetime, and there are still plenty of beaches. But tell me, where did the time go?

It seems as if it were only yesterday when I first found the special magic at The Stone, a place that for me has been symbolic of the passage of time and which I have known since my youth as a surfcaster. I am comfortable with the spot because I have been there many times when the tide was pulling to the east and felt the line straighten from the current. Just often enough, there has been a big striper there that has taken my offer and moved off.

The Stone is one of those special places that is reliable enough to make you want to go back; or, if you've been fishing the area, it is a place no competent surfcaster would want to pass up. Fact is, if the spot has any failing, it is that a few very good surfcasters know about it. Even nights when I had thoroughly scratched it, it always made me uneasy to see somebody come in late and test it for even a few casts. One never knew when a migrating striper might take it over. My selfish, overly possessive feelings about it bordered on the unhealthy—the idea of somebody else fishing *my* Stone!

Of course, it was not a spot that would hold only one fish. Once, on a big-water night during a new moon, a sou'west humping against the beach, big stripers were stacked in a current there, and I caught them until I ran out of eels. Only once. And that was so long ago; things were different then. That was before limits and concern for striper conservation.

I share a lot of memories with The Stone, but something— thanks to time—is changing our relationship. Many nights, on mid-watch hunts for striped bass, I resent each prod that the spot influences upon my memory. There is now something sad about The Stone, but not because it has changed. Enriched with the sensitivities of age, I am reminded by it all too well of a greater autumn than the one I am fishing.

I go to the spot much in the way another person might attend Mass. It is an almost unconscious acknowledgment of the seasons for me. In its inscrutable hold upon me, it is something of an altar of surfcasting that I am unaccountably compelled to respect, if for no other reason than an unrelenting past. There remains a here and now to each encounter with The Stone, but I am always visited by the memories that seem to inspire both an abiding sentimentality and extra effort. As always, the ritual remains a well-cast line with the express purpose of a fine striped bass.

Tonight, the ritual starts with a barely discernible change in wind, spitting snow in harmony with a drop in barometer and temperature. I know that I am shrugging off the season, immersed in some pretense, some inner conflict, that I'm really not supposed to care. And while there is cold in the night, the heat of summer lingers. I can feel the difference in my waders, see it from the sea smoke that hovers inches above the surface while the snow dances and darts into the gray fore.

The Stone is a good distance this year. Not that it ever moves, but the beach builds sand one year, takes it away another. There have been times when I could not reach it with an eel. Others, when it was too close, too accessible. This year, if I pressed my waders in a gentle surf, I picked up enough yardage to lay a bait far enough past it to be certain that I was covering it right. That is what I had done.

I wasn't bringing the eel in, just taking some of the line that the surf had left, when I felt a suspicious drum. Stepping forward so as to throw slack, I pushed the clutch, unconsciously positioning my right thumb to stop any override. The line lifted, then spun from the reel in long thrusts, as the take moved off in a series of erratic dashes. Then I engaged the gears, waited for the line to lift, and came back with the stick while stepping a yard backward with a shift in weight. There was some panic at the other end, a testing of what strange antagonism had beset it, then line moved against the drag.

Backing from the surf, I could feel the powerful surges of the lineside as its body straightened and flexed toward the outside against the line, as though something were whacking it. Dry braid left the spool now, but I felt no apprehension. Soon it would slow, trying a change in direction, and I would put it back on the reel. But now was the violent part, the time when the fish would test my equipment. It was important now to give it its way for a few minutes so it would tire and I could then take over. We had done this so many times that I was beginning to feel I was a character in a play, and that not even the fish had changed. The yards came easily; 2 left the spool grudgingly, the line's ownership shifting between us. The bass moved west along the beach a short distance while I followed, cranking. Then I made out the dorsal just outside, rising with each bulge in the sea. I pressured, the fin disappeared in a brief, spent struggle, and I hauled back gently just as the foam built and washed to shore. The oval form slid almost motionless in the white suds, and I kept it high long enough to ground it on the wet sand—then a few fast steps and a grasp of the lower jaw.

Years past, I might have unsheathed the rusty pick from my belt and pressed it into the lineside's skull, its pectorals extending briefly. Then I would have lifted the fish, carried it to where I had left my kit at the dune base, and buried it to keep anyone from seeing it. No more. Such rituals are as anachronistic as the gray-haired old man being watched from my boots. Lucky striper, it has resumed its freedom and migration.

This was a delicious time for me as I sat beside my things, my back against an eroding dune that slipped loose sand crackling against my parka. There was no need for another fish, I thought, while unwrapping a sandwich. The hot coffee burned a little, as if trying to fight an impending chill that might threaten this memorable time at the empty shore. Nothing on the outside, nothing in the sky. Even buggy tracks had been smoothed by the westerlies that were straining to change the seasons. I couldn't shake the feeling that there were two of us: a graying old man who struggled with the sea and another who could watch him as if exempt from all ravages while indulging in the joys of contemplation.

There might be another fish at The Stone, I thought, but if I quit now, I could leave with the feeling that I had triumphed over it again. I dared not risk languishing a winter in defeat. Walking down sans rod in one last ritualistic gesture, I watched a wave kiss the tip of The Stone. Trying to remember all that I could store, I savored the scent of rotting weed and salt, felt the last relative warmth of the water, heard the last rhythmic hiss of a season's surf while resisting the fearful urge to count remaining departures.

The silence of the snow, the loneliness of the shore, that last-man-on-earth feeling that I have known so many times before, never to be experienced again in quite the same way—it's something that you can never recreate in your mind. I know, because I have tried at night in bed when I foolishly sought to program my dreams. It is a drug that comes of its own calling, like the snow, where man has no control. I have thought of this many times, and I am certain that the only power we have is to go to the places where it is most likely to happen. I knew then, when I turned my face to the east and pulled my hood back to let the snow anoint me this one time more, that I was experiencing a feeling and a place so fleeting that I could never hope to have it quite the same way again.

Whipping my four-wheeler along the waterline trail toward dinner, my warm wife, and home, I thought of Devlin's Tap for a brandy and beer. Drafts are always so good in those old-time, little neighborhood taverns that date themselves with ladies' entrances. By now the snow was swirling so hard that it mingled white on white with the breaking surf. I thought of trying for another big fish, knowing that I could have made a thousand casts, landing who knows how many bass and blues, but the weather had me edgy, and I had had enough.

Once at Devlin's, I was beginning to think, it would be a certainty that some mackinaw-clad local cracker, part-way in his cups, noticing my waders and the snow, would stage-whisper that it takes all kinds. And I planned, because Lord knows I've done it many times before, to raise my glass in a subtle toast and wink at him for what he had missed.

PICK OF THE MONTH

Here is a calendar of hot spots:

February: Thames River (number 37)
March: Cape May (number 1)
April: Sound View Beach (number 34)
May: Sandy Hook Point (number 15)
June: Herring Run (number 71)
July: Race Point (number 83)
August: Popham Beach (number 97)
September: Plum Island (number 88)
October: Chatham Inlet (number 78)
November: Montauk Point (number 23)
December: Barnegat Inlet North Jetty (number 10)

BEST IN SPECIES

Here is a list of locations that are best for each of the following commonly sought species:

striped bass: Montauk Point (number 23)
bluefish: Wasque Point (number 62)
weakfish: Cape May (number 1)
blackfish: Orient Point (number 24)
fluke (summer flounder): Manasquan to Long Branch (number 14)
porgy (scup): East Beach (number 43)
bonito: Inlet to Great Salt Pond (number 60)
false albacore: Vineyard Bridges (number 61)

Porgy (scup) like these are easy to catch, provide fun for the family, and make a great fish fry. Best In Species for these is number 43, East Beach, Charlestown, R.I.

USUAL AND CUSTOMARY REQUIREMENTS FOR AN OVERSAND VEHICLE

The following items and accepted modes of behavior are usual for acquisition of permits to drive over sand. These requirements—sizes, strengths, and ratings—vary from one jurisdiction to another and are intended only to be representative of what is needed for a beach permit.

- Shovel (heavy duty military or entrenching)
- Tow rope or chain
- Jack and support stand
- Street-legal tires (snow or mud tread often rejected)
- Spare tire
- Low-pressure tire gauge (0–20 lbs.)
- First-aid kit (Coast Guard approved)
- Fire extinguisher (CG or ICC approved)
- Road flares
- Flashlight
- Auto insurance
- Four-wheel drive

All driving must be on prescribed dune trails or on the front beach.

Avoid bathing areas and other examples of user conflict.

Stay out of the dunes or any areas where vegetation might be compromised.

All beaches have speed limits, which vary from 5 to 15 m.p.h.

Ruts or holes caused by stuck vehicles must be filled and any debris removed.

No outside passengers (usually in the form of tailgate sitters).

Headlights must be used at all times.

Avoid bird nesting areas and stay out of marked areas.